MAXnotes®

Alex Haley's

The Autobiography of Malcolm X

Text by
Anita J. Aboulafia
(M.A., New York University)
ESL Department
New York Association for New Americans, Inc.
New York, New York

Illustrations by
Michael Kupka

Research & Education Association
Visit our website at
www.rea.com

Research & Education Association
61 Ethel Road West
Piscataway, New Jersey 08854
E-mail: info@rea.com

MAXnotes® for
THE AUTOBIOGRAPHY OF MALCOLM X

Published 2016

Printed in the United States of America

Library of Congress Control Number 2006927979

ISBN-13: 978-0-87891-004-5
ISBN-10: 0-87891-004-2

MAXnotes® and REA® are registered trademarks of
Research & Education Association, Inc.

What **MAXnotes**® *Will Do for You*

This book is intended to help you absorb the essential contents and features of Alex Haley's *The Autobiography of Malcolm X* and to help you gain a thorough understanding of the work. Our book has been designed to do this more quickly and effectively than any other study guide.

For best results, this **MAXnotes** book should be used as a companion to the actual work, not instead of it. The interaction between the two will greatly benefit you.

To help you in your studies, this book presents the most up-to-date interpretations of every section of the actual work, followed by questions and fully explained answers that will enable you to analyze the material critically. The questions also will help you to test your understanding of the work and will prepare you for discussions and exams.

Meaningful illustrations are included to further enhance your understanding and enjoyment of the literary work. The illustrations are designed to place you into the mood and spirit of the work's settings.

This **MAXnotes** book analyzes and summarizes each section as you go along, with discussions of the characters and explanations of the plot. A biography of the author and examination of the work's historical context will help you put this literary piece into the proper framework of what is taking place.

The use of this study guide will save you the hours of preparation time that would ordinarily be required to arrive at a complete grasp of this work of literature. You will be well prepared for classroom discussions, homework, and exams. The guidelines that are included for writing papers and reports on various topics will prepare you for any added work that may be assigned.

The **MAXnotes** will take your grades "to the max."

Larry B. Kling
Chief Editor

Contents

**Each chapter includes List of People,
Summary, Analysis, Study Questions and
Answers, and Suggested Essay Topics.**

SECTION ONE

Introduction

The Life and Work of Malcolm X

The Autobiography of Malcolm X is the remarkable true story of an African-American man's rise—from street hustler, dope peddler, and thief—to one of the most dynamic and influential African-American leaders in modern America. *The Autobiography of Malcolom X* spans four decades: from his birth on May 19, 1925 in Omaha, Nebraska, to his tragic assassination on February 21, 1965 in New York City.

As one of eight children of the Reverend Earl and Louise Little, Malcolm Little (as he was named at birth) grew up amidst poverty and racial prejudice. His father, the Reverend Little, was a Baptist minister and organizer for Marcus Garvey's UNIA (Universal Negro Improvement Association). As Garvey's disciple, the Reverend Little crusaded throughout the Midwest with his family, preaching and encouraging his congregations to return to their ancestral homeland, Africa.

In 1931, when Malcolm was six years old, his father was brutally murdered in Lansing, Michigan. Although never proven, it was believed that the Reverend Little had been killed by a local hate group. Life for the Little family changed drastically after that. Their financial problems worsened. In addition, Mrs. Little, suffering from enormous anxiety and stress caused by the responsibility of raising eight children, was eventually institutionalized. Consequently, in 1937, the Little children were separated; they lived with friends, foster families, or on their own in Lansing.

Malcolm attended school only through the eighth grade. He spent much of his teenage years on the streets of Boston, Chicago, and New York City's Harlem. In February 1946, at the age of 20, Malcolm was convicted of robbery and sentenced to a ten-year prison term. There he underwent a moral and spiritual transformation when he discovered the teachings of the Honorable Elijah Muhammad and the Nation of Islam. Known as the "Messenger of Allah" (Allah is the Muslim god), Muhammad instilled a sense of admiration and self-respect among his black followers by his condemnation of white people. He blamed whites for the abject conditions of black people in North America, and felt that the only way to resolve the longstanding injustices was through black separatism.

In 1953, upon his release from prison, Malcolm X (the name change "X" stood for his long-lost African name) was appointed assistant minister for the Nation of Islam movement. He traveled across the United States and eloquently preached about his new-found religion, converting thousands of black people.

In late 1963, Elijah Muhummad suspended Malcolm X from the Nation of Islam because of their differences on the fundamental precepts and strategies of the Black Muslims.

In 1964, Malcolm X made his first pilgrimage to Mecca. As a result of this visit, he established the Organization for Afro-American Unity, since he was determined to work proactively in the struggle for racial equality. Rather than adhere to the Nation of Islam's "non-engagement policy," Malcolm was intent on developing political strategies to combat America's racism.

Hostilities between Malcolm X and the Black Muslims heightened. He began receiving anonymous death threats.

On February 21, 1965, Malcolm X was assassinated. Although three men were convicted and sentenced to life imprisonment for his murder, the question of who ordered Malcolm X's assassination remains a mystery. Malcolm X is survived by his wife, Betty Shabazz, and four daughters.

In 1992, the African-American film director, Spike Lee, made a film, *Malcolm X,* based on *The Autobiography of Malcolm X.* Denzel Washington portrayed Malcolm X in this critically-acclaimed motion picture.

The Life and Work of Alex Haley

Alex Haley (August 11, 1921–February 10, 1992) was a chief journalist in the U.S. Coast Guard for 20 years before he began his civilian writing career. He first wrote about the Nation of Islam movement in 1960 in a *Reader's Digest* article. Subsequently, he was introduced to Malcolm X and conducted a personal interview with him for an article for *Playboy* magazine. The *Playboy* interview was the inspiration for *The Autobiography of Malcolm X*. This bestselling classic was a culmination of nearly two years of intensive interviews.

Mr. Haley won literary fame for his exhaustively researched book on his family's history, *Roots: The Saga of an American Family* (1976). Winner of the Pulitzer Prize, the book traces his maternal ancestry back to Africa.

Mr. Haley wrote stories and articles for numerous publications and published a novella, *A Different Kind of Christmas*, in 1988.

Historical Background

The Autobiography of Malcolm X chronicles four decades—from the 1920s to the 1960s—of America's social, political, and economic climates. Up to the mid-1950s, racial segregation was legal. Neighborhoods, schools, and all types of businesses were segregated. A 1955 Supreme Court ruling declared school segregation illegal, by stating that "separate but equal is inherently unequal."

In addition, several states, particularly in the South, demanded a "poll tax" of African-Americans as a means of preventing them from voting in elections. It was only with the passage of the 24th Amendment to the U.S. Constitution, in 1962, that this poll tax became illegal.

All Americans experienced grave hardships during the Great Depression, which started in 1929 and lasted through the 1930s. The effects on African-Americans were especially devastating, given their already inferior status in American society.

By the 1950s, an organized black militancy had emerged—both violent and nonviolent—in which Malcolm X played a pivotal role. He believed that African-Americans had a right and a duty to defend themselves, by any means necessary, against the violence directed at them by the white power structure (which he believed to be racist), and by racist vigilante groups (such as the Ku Klux Klan). Furthermore, he criticized the various civil rights organizations and civil rights leaders (for example, the Reverend Martin Luther King, Jr.),who sought a peaceful solution to America's racial problems.

Toward the end of his life, Malcolm X moderated his views. He advocated African-American solidarity, and urged people of all races to work together to end America's racism.

Master List of People

Malcolm Little—*the narrator and main character.*

Louise Little—*Malcolm's mother.*

The Reverend Earl Little—*Malcolm's father, a Baptist minister.*

Yvonne—*Malcolm's youngest sister.*

Robert—*Malcolm's younger brother.*

Philbert—*Malcolm's older brother.*

Wilfred—*Malcolm's older brother.*

Hilda—*Malcolm's older sister.*

Reginald—*Malcolm's younger brother.*

Wesley—*Malcolm's younger brother.*

The Gohannas—*a family with whom the young Malcolm goes to live.*

Big Boy—*the Gohannas' nephew.*

Mrs. Adcock—*a woman who lives with the Gohannas.*

Bill Peterson—*white boxer who fights Malcolm.*

Maynard Allen—*works for the state welfare agency.*

Mr. and Mrs. Swerlin—*a white couple in charge of detention home.*

Lucille Lathrop—*white cook-helper who works for the Swerlins.*

Duane Lathrop—*Lucille's husband.*

A judge—*in charge of Malcolm's case in Lansing.*

Mr. and Mrs. Lyons—*a West Indian couple whose children attend school with Malcolm.*

Mr. Ostrowski—*Malcolm's English teacher.*

Mr. Williams—*Malcolm's history teacher.*

Ella—*Malcolm's half-sister who lives in Boston.*

Earl—*Malcolm's half-brother.*

Mary—*Malcolm's half-sister.*

Frank—*Ella's second husband.*

Audrey Slaugh—*Malcolm's classmate.*

Jimmy Cotton—*Malcolm's classmate.*

Shorty—*Malcolm's friend.*

Freddie—*works as a shoeshine boy.*

Laura—*a black high school honors student.*

Mamie Bevels—*waitress at Roseland.*

Sophia—*a white girl Malcolm meets at Roseland.*

Old Man Rountree—*elderly Pullman porter and friend of Ella's.*

Pappy Cousins—*Yankee Clipper steward.*

Ed Small—*owner of Small's Paradise, a popular Harlem nightspot.*

Charlie Small—*Ed's brother, who interviews Malcolm for a job.*

The Forty Thieves—*a group of men who steal clothing from stores and resell at one-third of the store's prices.*

The Four Horsemen—*a group of crooked black policemen who patrol Harlem's Sugar Hill neighborhood.*

Brisbane—*a West Indian policeman.*

"Cadillac" Drake—a *Harlem pimp.*

Sammy the Pimp—*a pimp and close friend of Malcolm's.*

"Alabama Peach"—*a white prostitute who works for Sammy.*

"Dollarbill"—*a Harlem pimp.*

"Fewclothes"—*a former pickpocket and regular customer at Small's Paradise.*

"Jumpsteady"—*a burglar and regular at Small's Paradise.*

Creole Bill—*Malcolm's friend, who converts his apartment into a speakeasy.*

"Brown Sugar"—*Creole Bill's girlfriend.*

"St. Louis Red"—*an armed robber whom Malcolm once worked with.*

"Chicago Red"—*a funny dishwasher; later he will become famous as Redd Foxx.*

Joe Baker—*a West Indian plainclothes New York City detective.*

Gladys Hampton—*wife of famed musician, Lionel Hampton.*

Frank Schiffman—*owner of the Apollo Theater.*

West Indian Archie—*a numbers runner in Harlem.*

Hymie—*a Jewish restaurant owner whom Malcolm works for.*

Jean Parks—*a former singer and friend of Malcolm's.*

Billie Holliday—*a famous black jazz singer.*

Sophia's 17-year old sister—*is unnamed throughout the autobiography; dates Shorty.*

White lesbian and her girlfriend—*Malcolm's friends.*

John Hughes—*owns a gambling house in Boston.*

Rudy—*a friend of Shorty's and member of Malcolm's burglary ring.*

Turner—*one of Boston's two black police detectives.*

Sophia's husband—*goes looking for Malcolm when he discovers that Sophia has been dating him.*

Sophia's husband's friend—*takes Sophia and her sister out to dinner.*

Detective Slack—*police detective who investigates Malcolm.*

Detective Turner—*police detective who investigates Malcolm.*

Spanish Negro Woman—*Sammy's girlfriend.*

Bimbi—*Malcolm's fellow inmate in Charlestown State Prison, who encourages Malcolm to take prison correspondence courses.*

The Honorable Elijah Muhammad—*the leader of the Nation of Islam.*

"Mr. Yacub"—*According to the teachings of Elijah Muhammad, this black man created the white race 6,600 years ago.*

Master W.D. Fard—*a half-black, half-white man who gave Elijah Muhammad Allah's message and divine guidance.*

Lemuel Hassan—*minister of Detroit's Temple Number One.*

Sister Clara Muhammad—*Elijah Muhammad's wife.*

Mother Marie—*Elijah Muhammad's mother.*

Brother Lloyd X—*a Muslim follower in Boston.*

Brother Osborne—*a Muslim follower in Springfield, Massachusetts.*

Brother James X—*a Muslim follower in Atlanta, Georgia.*

Sister Betty X—*Malcolm's wife.*

Brother John Ali and his wife—*a couple who share a house with Malcolm and his wife in Queens, New York.*

Louis Lomax—*black journalist who profiles the Nation of Islam in a television documentary.*

Professor C. Eric Lincoln—*black scholar who writes a book about the Nation of Islam.*

James Hicks—*editor of the* Amsterdam News, *a Harlem newspaper.*

Various Brothers and Sisters—*followers of Muhammad's Nation of Islam.*

Dr. Leana A. Turner—*Malcolm's family doctor.*

Cassius Clay—*famous Muslim heavyweight boxer.*

Sonny Liston—*famous heavyweight boxer who fights Cassius Clay.*

Floyd Patterson—*famous heavyweight boxer who fights Cassius Clay.*

Wallace Muhammad—*Elijah Muhammad's son.*

Dr. Mahmoud Youssef Shawarbi—*a Muslim lecturer, writer, professor, and United Nations' advisor, and close advisor to Prince Faisal, who helps Malcolm make his pilgrimage to Mecca.*

Prince Faisal—*the ruler of Saudi Arabia.*

Abd ir-Rahman Azzam—*author of* The Eternal Message of Muhammad, *who lives in Jedda* .

Muhammad Shawarbi—*son of Dr. Shawarbi; a student at Cairo University.*

Dr. Omar Azzam—*son of Mr. Azzam, and a Swiss-trained engineer who lives in Jedda.*

Muhammad, the Mutawaf—*a young man who serves as a guide to Malcolm on his pilgrimage to Mecca.*

Hussein Amini, the Grand Mufti of Jerusalem—*a Muslim leader.*

Sheikh Muhammad Harkon—*judge of the Muslim High Court.*

Kasem Gulek—*member of the Turkish Parliament who Malcolm meets on Mount Arafat.*

Sheikh Abdullah Eraif—*mayor of Mecca.*

Muhammad Abdul Azziz Maged—*Saudi Arabia's Deputy Chief of Protocol, who serves as an interpreter for conversations between Malcolm and Prince Faisal.*

Professor Essien-Udom—*author of* Black Nationalism, *and professor at Ibadan University in Lagos, Nigeria.*

Larry Jackson—*Black Peace Corps' volunteer whom Malcolm meets in Nigeria.*

Julian Mayfield—*author and leader of Ghana's group of African-American expatriates.*

Ana Livia—*Mayfield's wife.*

Dr. Kwame Nkrumah—*President of Ghana.*

Shirley Graham Du Bois—*writer and director of Ghanaian television; widow of famous African-American revolutionary and scholar, Dr. W.E.B. Du Bois, who moved to Ghana late in his life.*

Alex Haley—*the person to whom Malcolm tells his autobiography, and writer of the autobiography's epilogue.*

Ossie Davis—*popular actor and friend of Malcolm, who eulogized Malcolm.*

Reverend Milton Galamison—*militant clergyman, who was sched-*

*uled to be the co-speaker with Malcolm at the Audubon Ball-
room on the day Malcolm was assassinated.*

Brother Benjamin X—*Malcolm's assistant at the Muslim Mosque,
Inc.*

Stanley Scott—*United Press International reporter who was at the
Audubon Ballroom when Malcolm was assassinated.*

Bishop Alvin A. Childs—*Malcolm's funeral was held at his church,
Church of God in Christ.*

Summary of the Autobiography

The Autobiography of Malcolm X as told to Alex Haley
chronicles the rise of Malcolm X, from his years as a street hustler,
dope peddler, and thief to becoming one of the most influential
African-American leaders in the American civil rights' movement.

Journalist Alex Haley first approached Malcolm X about writing his autobiography in 1963. The autobiography was a culmination of nearly two years of intensive interviews with Malcolm X,
which concluded in 1965 after his tragic assassination.

The autobiography traces Malcolm's early years in Michigan,
where he was one of eight children of the Reverend Earl and Louise
Little. By 1937, when Malcolm was 12 years old, his father had been
brutally murdered and his mother institutionalized.

Malcolm vividly recounts his teenage years, spent in Boston,
Chicago, and New York City's Harlem. The reader enters Malcolm's
world of street hustlers and pimps, and witnesses the devastating
effects racial segregation and prejudice had on African-Americans
in the 1940s and 1950s.

In 1946, Malcolm is sentenced to a 10-year prison term for robbery. It is in prison where he undergoes a moral and spiritual transformation, after he discovers the teaching of the Honorable Elijah
Muhammad and his Nation of Islam. For the first time in his life,
Malcolm studies and learns about the proud history and traditions
of black people throughout the world. According to Elijah
Muhammad, white people are "devils" because they have oppressed and exploited black people for centuries. Elijah Muhammad believed that black separatism was the only way to resolve
the problem of racism in America.

Malcolm decides to devote his life to spreading the teachings of Elijah Muhammad. Upon his release from prison in 1953, Malcolm moves to Detroit and initiates a Nation of Islam recruitment drive. Soon, he is traveling across the United States, electrifying his audiences as he eloquently preaches about the Nation of Islam movement.

Malcolm's marriage to Betty Shabazz in 1958 is a joyful time; he and his wife move to Queens, New York.

The reader is aware of Malcolm's growing disenchantment with the Nation of Islam movement. Malcolm wants the movement to take a more activist role in combatting America's racism. Meanwhile, Malcolm senses that Elijah Muhammad has become jealous of his enormous popularity. This jealousy, in fact, leads Muhammad to begin distancing himself from Malcolm.

Finally, when Elijah Muhammad silences Malcolm for 90 days, Malcolm decides to create a new organization, substantially different from the Nation of Islam, that will fight America's racism with political activism.

Malcolm makes two pilgrimages to the holy city of Mecca. There, he is amazed by the true sense of "brotherhood" practiced by people of all races and nationalities. As a result of his spiritual awakening, he renounces his black separatist beliefs.

The book's Epilogue details the tragic assassination of 39-year-old Malcolm X. Haley writes that although it has never been proven, most people believe that Black Muslims were responsible for Malcolm's death.

Estimated Reading Time

The average silent reading rate for a secondary student is 250 to 300 words per minute. Since each page has approximately 400 words on it, an average student would take about two minutes to read each page. The total reading time for the 460-page book would be about 16 hours. Reading the book according to the natural chapter breaks is the best approach.

The Autobiography of Malcolm X

Chapter 1: Nightmare

New People:

Malcolm Little: *the narrator and main character*

Louise Little: *Malcolm's mother*

The Reverend Earl Little: *Malcolm's father, a Baptist minister*

Yvonne: *Malcolm's youngest sister*

Robert: *Malcolm's younger brother*

Philbert: *Malcolm's older brother*

Wilfred: *Malcolm's older brother*

Hilda: *Malcolm's older sister*

Reginald: *Malcolm's younger brother*

Wesley: *Malcolm's younger brother*

The Gohannas: *a family with whom the young Malcolm goes to live*

Big Boy: *the Gohannas' nephew*

Mrs. Adcock: *a woman who lived with the Gohannas*

Summary

The first chapter begins in 1926 and chronicles the first eleven years of Malcolm's life with his hard-working parents and seven siblings. It describes the tragic murder of his father, Malcolm's first brush with petty crime, and the eventual break-up of the Little family when his mother is institutionalized.

Analysis

Malcolm's memories of his childhood are brutally honest. His father's unwavering belief in the importance of self-reliance and his willingness to risk his life preaching revolutionary, back-to-Africa sermons had a profound influence on young Malcolm. In addition, he learns an important life lesson during his rabbit-hunting expedition with Mr. Gohannas and his friends. Malcolm's strategizes and shoots many more rabbits than his companions. He concludes, "Anytime you find someone more successful than you are, especially when you're both engaged in the same business—you know they're doing something that you aren't." The title of the chapter, "Nightmare," conjures up a dark and forboding image. It forewarns the reader that something evil is about to happen. Indeed, in the first sentence, the narrator, Malcolm, gives a chilling description of "hooded Ku Klux Klan riders" who "galloped up to our home in Omaha, Nebraska, one night." Later on, Malcolm's mother has a premonition about her husband's impending murder, but she is powerless to prevent it. The final nightmare in the chapter occurs when, in Malcolm's words, "our family was destroyed." Here, Malcolm is distraught because his mother has been committed to a state mental hospital, and the Little family is separated.

Paradoxically, the style Malcolm uses to describe his childhood tragedies is straightforward and surprisingly dispassionate. As Malcolm recounts his father's vicious murder, for example, he reports, "My father's skull, on one side, was crushed in. . . . His body was cut almost in half. He lived two and a half hours in that condition. Negroes then were stronger than they are now, especially Georgia Negroes." Here, although Malcolm is grief-stricken, he has emotionally distanced himself from this early trauma.

This first chapter sets the mood and tone for the rest of the autobiography. The reader can presume that Malcolm's innocent and carefree days have been lost forever. His inner confict, the choice between leading a life of crime or following in the footsteps of his illustrious father, recurs throughout the book.

Study Questions

1. Where were Malcolm's parents from?

2. What was the Black Legion?

3. Where did Reverend Little keep his pistol?

4. Why did Malcolm think that his father favored him over his other children?

5. Why was the Little family "better off" than most black families in East Lansing, Michigan?

6. Why did one insurance company refuse to pay off the life insurance policy of Reverend Little?

7. What strategic lesson did Malcolm learn from his rabbit-hunting expedition?

8. Why did Malcolm like to visit the Gohannas family?

9. How did Malcolm feel about his older sister Hilda?

10. How long did Louise Little remain in the state mental hospital in Kalamazoo, Michigan?

Answers

1. Malcolm's father was from Reynolds, Georgia and his mother was from Grenada, in the British West Indies.

2. The Black Legion was a hate society of white racists in Lansing, Michigan.

3. Reverend Little's pistol was hidden, kept sewn up in a pillow.

4. Malcolm thought that his father favored him because he was his father's lightest-colored child. He felt that his father had been subconsciously brainwashed by white men into preferring lighter-skinned blacks.

5. The Little family built a small house in East Lansing, Michigan and raised much of their own food.

6. The insurance company claimed that Reverend Little had committed suicide and refused to pay off his life insurance policy.

7. Malcolm learned that any time you find someone more successful than you are, especially when you are both engaged in the same business, that person is doing something that you aren't.

8. Malcolm liked to visit the Gohannas family because his own family had become destitute. Whenever he dropped by, they would invite him to stay for dinner.

9. Malcolm considered his older sister to be his second mother.

10. Louise Little remained in the state mental hospital for about 26 years.

Suggested Essay Topics

1. Malcolm describes the racial prejudice in Lansing, Michigan. Give three examples of this prejudice and explain the negative psychological impact such prejudice could have on black people.

2. How did Malcolm psychologically cope with the death of his father?

Chapter 2: Mascot

New People:

Bill Peterson: *white boxer who fights Malcolm*

Maynard Allen: *works for the state welfare agency*

Mr. and Mrs. Swerlin: *a white couple in charge of the detention home*

Lucille Lathrop: *white cook-helper who works for the Swerlins*

Duane Lathrop: *Lucille's husband*

A judge: *in charge of Malcolm's case in Lansing*

Mr. and Mrs. Lyons: *a West Indian couple whose children attend school with Malcolm*

Mr. Ostrowski: *Malcolm's English teacher*

Mr. Williams: *Malcolm's history teacher*

Ella: *Malcolm's half-sister who lives in Boston*

Earl: *Malcolm's half-brother*

Mary: *Malcolm's half-sister*

Frank: *Ella's second husband*

Audrey Slaugh: *Malcolm's classmate*

Jimmy Cotton: *Malcolm's classmate*

Summary

At the age of 13, Malcolm is expelled from school in Lansing, Michigan because of his misbehavior. He is sent to live in a detention home in the neighboring city of Mason. Mr. and Mrs. Swerlin like Malcolm very much. Mrs. Swerlin finds an afterschool job for Malcolm in a local restaurant. He achieves academic success in the white junior high school he attends, and participates in several afterschool activities. Thanks to his popularity, he is elected class president.

Malcolm's half-sister from Boston, Ella, visits the Little family. A "leading light" in Boston's "black society," Ella invites Malcolm to Boston in the summer of 1940. When he visits Boston, 15-year-old Malcolm is amazed by the bustling black community of Roxbury, where Ella and her husband live.

Upon his return to Mason, Malcolm becomes increasingly dissatisfied and restless, and misses that strong sense of belonging that he experienced in Roxbury. People begin to notice a change in him. His disillusionment with Mason grows after a conversation he has with Mr. Ostrowski. During that conversation, Malcolm

told Ostrowski that he aspired to become a lawyer. Despite Malcolm's academic achievements, Ostrowski advised him against pursuing this profession, saying, "A lawyer—that's no realistic goal for a nigger." Rather, Ostrowski suggested that Malcolm become a carpenter.

Malcolm writes to Ella, saying that he would like to come live with her in Boston. As the chapter concludes, Ella receives official custody of Malcolm, and he moves to Boston.

Analysis

In Mason, Malcolm lives and attends school with white people. He is accepted by them, not as an equal, but—as the chapter's title asserts—as a "mascot." The Swerlins refer to black people as "niggers" and continually make derogatory remarks about them. Malcolm asserts, "It just never dawned upon them [the Swerlins]...that I wasn't a pet, but a human being."

Throughout the chapter, Malcolm has a sharp eye for detail, and uses similes and metaphors to describe how white people perceive him. He says, "He [a white judge] would look me up and down, his expression approving, like he was examining a fine colt, or a pedigreed pup."

Malcolm is angry and resentful of white people's condescending attitudes. Nonetheless, he initially feels helpless in the face of such adversity. Finally, when his teacher attempts to dissuade him from pursuing a career as a lawyer, Malcolm's emerging self-confidence and maturity enable him to write to Ella, requesting that he come there to live.

Malcolm's decision to move to Boston is the first major turning point in his life. It represents the first time that he has felt empowered to improve his circumstances. In retrospect, as Malcolm describes the implications of his decision, he says, "No physical move in my life has been more pivotal or profound in its repercussions."

Study Questions

1. What was the outcome of Malcolm's boxing matches with Bill Peterson?

2. Why was Malcolm expelled from school?

3. In what extracurricular activities did Malcolm participate in Mason Junior High School?

4. Where did Malcolm work after school?

5. What were Malcolm's favorite subjects in school?

6. What did Malcolm think was unique about his half-sister Ella?

7. How did Ella become financially successful?

8. How did Malcolm feel after Ella's suggestion about the Little family visiting their mother? Why?

9. What professions did Mr. Ostrowski encourage Malcolm's classmates to pursue?

10. Where did Malcolm go to listen to music when he visited Boston?

Answers

1. Bill Peterson won both boxing matches.

2. Malcolm was expelled because he placed a thumbtack on his teacher's chair.

3. Malcolm was a member of the debating society and the junior high basketball team.

4. Malcolm worked in a local restaurant, washing dishes.

5. Malcolm's favorite subjects were English and history.

6. Malcolm felt that his half-sister Ella was "the first really proud black woman" he had ever seen in his life.

7. Ella became financially successful by investing in real estate.

8. Malcolm was grateful and optimistic about Ella's suggestion because he felt that she could help his mother get well and return to her family.

9. Mr. Ostrowski encouraged Malcolm's classmates to pursue careers as teachers, a county agent, a veterinarian, and a nurse.

10. Malcolm went to the Roseland State Ballroom in Boston to listen to music.

Suggested Essay Topics

1. What were Mr. Williams' (Malcolm's history teacher) views on black history? Explain.

2. Malcolm says that if he hadn't moved to Boston he would "still be a brainwashed black Christian." Explain.

Chapter 3: "Homeboy"

New People:

Shorty: *Malcolm's friend*

Freddie: *works as a shoeshine boy*

Summary

Malcolm lives with Ella and her family in an area known as "the Hill" in Roxbury, a large black neighborhood in Boston. Most black people residing in the Hill are servants, or have other types of menial employment; a small number are white-collar workers.

Shorty helps Malcolm get a job shining shoes at the Roseland State Ballroom. Malcolm soon discovers that shoeshining is only part of the job. His additional responsibilities include selling liquor, marijuana, and pimping. He develops a taste for Roxbury's black urban fashion and lifestyle. He purchases his first "zoot suit," and begins "conking," or straightening, his hair. He spends his free time shooting craps, playing cards, drinking, and smoking marijuana with Shorty and his friends.

Analysis

In this chapter, Malcolm undergoes his first transformation—from a "country" boy to a big city "hipster." However, it is ironic that his vivid descriptions of this black urban culture of zoot suits and dancing are sharp contrasts to the lurking evils that are undeniably present—of illegal drugs, gambling, and prostitution.

Toward the end of the chapter, Malcolm acknowledges, in hindsight, the irony of this seemingly happy period of his life. He says that when he was a teenager living in Roxbury, he felt proud that this black community had its own, distinct cultural identity. He realizes, however, in retrospect, the enormous influence white people's culture actually had over black people at that time. When discussing his "conked" hair, for example, Malcolm shamefully admits, "I had joined that multitude of Negro men and women in America who are brainwashed into believing that the black people are 'inferior'—and white people 'superior'—that they will even violate and mutilate their God-created bodies to try to look 'pretty' by white standards."

The reader, of course, has the foresight to recognize that Malcolm's experiences—whether positive or negative—are all part of his growth process. Malcolm's remarkable journey will eventually lead him to achieve great personal satisfaction and fulfillment.

Study Questions

1. What does Ella want Malcolm to do when he arrives in Boston?

2. Who was Crispus Attucks?

3. What instrument does Shorty play?

4. What is a "slave"?

5. What was Malcolm's first job in Boston?

6. Name four famous black jazz musicians who performed at Roseland.

7. What type of car does Freddie drive?

8. What is the first item that Malcolm buys on credit?

9. What is a "conk"?

10. What ingredients are necessary in order to conk one's hair?

Answers

1. Ella wants Malcolm to get to know the city by walking around and traveling through it.

2. Crispus Attucks was a Negro and the first American patriot to be killed by the British in the Boston Massacre.

3. Shorty plays the saxophone.

4. A "slave" is a slang word for a job.

5. Malcolm's first job in Boston was shining shoes at the Roseland State Ballroom.

6. The famous black jazz musicians who perform at Roseland include Duke Ellington, Count Basie, Lionel Hampton, Cootie Williams, Jimmie Lunceford, Johnny Hodges, Sonny Greer, Jimmie Rushing, Lester Young, Harry Edison, Buddy Tate, Don Byas, Dickie Wells, and Buck Clayton.

7. Freddie drives a pearl gray Cadillac.

8. The first item Malcolm buys on credit is a zoot suit.

9. A "conk" is a slang term for a hairstyle created when African-Americans straighten their hair with lye.

10. The ingredients necessary to conk one's hair are a can of Red Devil lye, two eggs, and two potatoes.

Suggested Essay Topics

1. Boston's black neighborhood, Roxbury, is divided into two distinct areas—the "Hill" and the "town." How were these areas different?

2. How does Malcolm feel about Shorty? Explain.

Chapter 4: Laura

New People:

Laura: *a black high school honors student*

Mamie Bevels: *waitress at Roseland*

Sophia: *a white girl Malcolm meets at Roseland*

Summary

Dancing becomes Malcolm's first and foremost passion. He quits his shoeshining job and takes a job as a soda fountain clerk, enabling him to go out dancing at night. At work, he meets Laura, a sheltered black girl living with her grandmother. He takes Laura dancing at Roseland and the two are a dancing sensation.

Malcolm stops dating Laura after he meets an attractive, wealthy white woman he refers to as Sophia. Meanwhile, Laura's life drastically changes. In defiance of her grandmother, she starts drinking liquor and using dope; soon, she becomes a prostitute to support her drug habit. Laura hates her male customers and, subsequently, becomes a lesbian. Ultimately, she spends time in and out of jail.

Financed by Sophia, Malcolm moves in with Shorty. He begins to work as a bus boy at Boston's Parker House.

The chapter concludes as Malcolm learns that the Japanese have just bombed Pearl Harbor.

Analysis

The reader is totally immersed in the culture and lifestyle of Roxbury's black community. Malcolm begins using "hip" slang terms to describe his experiences and the people he encounters. Comparing himself to a "dancing jigaboo" toy, he says, "I met chicks who were fine as May wine, and cats who were hip to all happenings."

As Malcolm easily adapts to the culture of Roxbury's black community, his status is further enhanced by his relationship with a white woman.

Significantly, Malcolm has called this chapter, "Laura." To the reader, Laura emerges as a figure who plays a relatively minor role in his life. However, Malcolm admits, "One of the shames I have carried for years is that I blame myself for all of this [Laura's prostitution and eventual downfall]. To have treated her as I did for a white woman made the blow doubly heavy." Thus, Laura serves as an ugly reminder to Malcolm of his own moral and physical deterioration during this period of his life.

Study Questions

1. How does Ella feel when Malcolm quits his shoeshining job? Why?

2. What is Shorty's career goal?

3. What does Malcolm do the day after he quits his shoeshining job?

4. Where does Malcolm work as a soda fountain clerk?

5. Where do Malcolm and Laura go on their first date?

6. What band is playing the second time Laura and Malcolm go to Roseland?

7. Where do Sophia and Malcolm go on dates?

8. What is a "rubber"?

9. How does Shorty feel about Sophia?

10. How does Ella feel about Sophia?

Answers

1. Ella is glad when Malcolm quits his shoeshining job because she feels that the job had no prestige.

2. Shorty wants to start his own musical group and perform around Boston.

3. The day after he quits his shoeshining job, Malcolm buys another zoot suit and gets his first barbershop conk.

4. Malcolm is a soda fountain clerk at Townsend Drug Store.

5. Malcolm and Laura go to a dance at the Roseland Ballroom on their first date.

6. The Duke Ellington band is playing the second time Laura and Malcolm go to Roseland.

7. Sophia and Malcolm go to dances and bars around Roxbury.

8. A rubber is a slang word for a car.

9. Shorty likes Sophia very much.

10. Ella does not like Sophia at all.

Suggested Essay Topics

1. Malcolm becomes friends with Shorty and Laura. Compare and contrast these two people.

2. Malcolm takes great pride in his relationship with Sophia. Explain.

Chapter 5: Harlemite

New People:

Old Man Rountree: *elderly Pullman porter and friend of Ella's*

Pappy Cousins: *Yankee Clipper steward*

Ed Small: *owner of Small's Paradise, a popular Harlem nightspot*

Charlie Small: *Ed's brother, who interviews Malcolm for a job*

Summary

In 1942, Malcolm is hired by a railroad company to work as a dishwasher on its Boston to Washington, DC run. Soon, he is promoted and begins selling food on the "Yankee Clipper," the train that runs between Boston and New York City. On his first trip to New York's Harlem, he visits several nightclubs and sees such famous black celebrities as Dizzy Gillespie and Ella Fitzgerald. Immediately deciding that "this world was where I belonged," he becomes a regular at Harlem's hottest nightspots.

Meanwhile, Malcolm is fired by the railroad company after they receive complaints from people about his rude behavior. Confident that he will find another job—however menial—easily because of America's booming wartime economy, Malcolm pays a visit to his family in Lansing. His conked, fire-red hair and zoot suits create a sensation there.

Back in New York, Malcolm becomes a day waiter at Small's Paradise. He learns about Harlem's long history as a safe haven for the vast numbers of immigrants—Dutch, German, and Irish, to name a few—who once resided in Harlem. In addition, he discovers how Harlem gained its notoriety—the numbers hustling, pimping, dope peddling, and thievery.

Analysis

This chapter vividly illustrates the prevailing racial climate of the early 1940s. America's black people were economically and socially disadvantaged. Resentment and anger were slowly building up in black communities. Thus, the reader must regard Malcolm's behavior within the context of such attitudes.

Malcolm, like many young black men during World War II, does not want to join the army. He agrees with Shorty, who, explaining his reluctance to serve in the army, says, "Whitey owns everything. He wants us to go and bleed for him? Let him fight."

It is, however, necessary for black people to maintain cordial relationships with white people. White people are often their employers, or the people to whom one must show respect. Malcolm encounters white people when he sells food on the railroad. He credits his success at this job to his submissive, "Uncle Tomming" antics, which earn him bigger tips. He perceptively notes, "We were in that world of Negroes who are both servants and psychologists, aware that white people are so obsessed with their own importance that they will pay liberally, even dearly, for the impression of being catered to and entertained." Evidently, he is willing to demean himself in order to get higher tips.

Later on, Malcolm cleverly humiliates a white passenger. A drunken white soldier, referring to Malcolm as "nigger," challenges him to a fist fight. Malcolm responds, "Sure, I'll fight, but you've got too many clothes on." The drunken sailor proceeds to disrobe

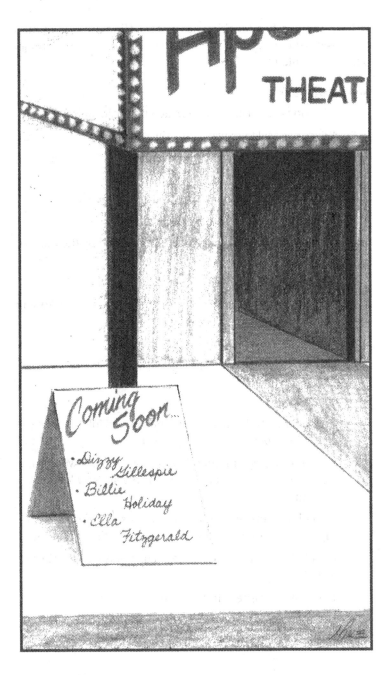

in front of the other, laughing passengers. Ultimately, Malcolm's anger—at white people in general—has led him to take revenge against this soldier.

Study Questions

1. Why does Ella recommend Malcolm for the railroad job?

2. Why does Malcolm want the railroad job?

3. What is surprising to Malcolm when he visits Washington, DC?

4. Where does Malcolm stay on his first visit to Harlem?

5. What is Malcolm's favorite drink?

6. Why isn't Malcolm worried after being fired by the railroad company?

7. Who does Malcolm visit in Kalamazoo, Michigan?

8. What is Malcolm's first job when he moves to New York in 1942?

9. When did Harlem's Cotton Club open?

10. Where does the "Lindy Hop" get its name?

Answers

1. Ella recommends Malcolm for the railroad job because she wants him to move out of Boston and stop dating Sophia.

2. Malcolm wants a railroad job because the job would provide him with free transportation to visit New York City's Harlem.

3. Malcolm is surprised to find thousands of poor people living just a few blocks from Capitol Hill and the White House.

4. On his first visit to Harlem, Malcolm stays at the Harlem YMCA.

5. Malcolm's favorite drink is a shot of bourbon.

6. Malcolm wasn't worried after being fired because, during America's war years, the economy was very strong.

7. Malcolm visits his mother, who is in a state hospital in Kalamazoo, Michigan.

8. Malcolm's first job in New York City is as a day waiter in Small's Paradise.

9. Harlem's Cotton Club opened in 1926.

10. The Lindy Hop is named after Charles Lindburgh, an aviator who made an historic, nonstop flight from New York to Paris in 1927.

Suggested Essay Topics

1. When Malcolm sells food on the railroad, he asserts, "All you had to do was give white people a show and they'd buy anything you offered them." Explain his theory.

2. Malcolm says he was "mesmerized" the first time he visited Harlem. What does "mesmerized" mean? Why does Malcolm feel this way?

Chapter 6: Detroit Red
Chapter 7: Hustler

New People:

The Forty Thieves: *a group of men who steal clothing from stores to resell at one-third of the store's prices*

The Four Horsemen: *a group of crooked black policemen who patrol Harlem's Sugar Hill neighborhood*

Brisbane: *a West Indian policeman who is one of The Four Horsemen*

"Cadillac" Drake: *a Harlem pimp*

Sammy the Pimp: *a pimp and best friend of Malcolm*

"Alabama Peach": *a white prostitute who works for Sammy*

"Dollarbill": *a Harlem pimp*

"Fewclothes": *a former pickpocket and regular customer at Small's Paradise*

"Jumpsteady": *a burglar and regular customer at Small's Paradise*

Creole Bill: *Malcolm's friend, who converts his apartment into a speakeasy*

"Brown Sugar": *Creole Bill's girlfriend*

"St. Louis Red": *a professional armed robber whom Malcolm once worked with*

"Chicago Red": *a funny dishwasher; later he will become famous as Redd Foxx*

Billie Holiday: *the famous black jazz singer*

Spanish Negro Woman: *Sammy's girlfriend*

White lesbian and her girlfriend: *friends of Malcolm*

Joe Baker: *a West Indian plainclothes New York City detective*

Gladys Hampton: *wife of famed musician, Lionel Hampton*

Frank Schiffman: *owner of the Apollo Theater*

West Indian Archie: *a numbers runner in Harlem*

Hymie: *a Jewish restaurant owner whom Malcolm works for*

Jean Parks: *a former singer and friend of Malcolm*

Summary

In Chapters 6 and 7, Malcolm describes his Harlem lifestyle in great detail. Nicknamed "Detroit Red," he supports himself by working in Small's Paradise, and engages in such extracurricular activities as gambling, hustling, and using drugs. He lives amongst prostitutes and drug users, and befriends pimps. Although she has gotten married, Sophia continues visiting Malcolm. One day, while at work, he is arrested by the police for giving an undercover cop the telephone number of a prostitute. Although he is freed by the police for lack of evidence, he loses his waiter job and, with the help of Sammy the Pimp, begins peddling marijuana.

He visits Ella, Sophia, and Shorty in Boston. Shorty now has his own band and is playing in small clubs.

White narcotics detectives start harassing Malcolm, so he gets an automatic pistol for protection. As a result of his continued paranoia about being followed by the detectives, he begins to commute on railroad lines, selling marijuana to traveling musicians.

Upon his return to Harlem, he receives a draft notice. When he reports to the army induction center, he pretends to be psychotic by threatening to kill white soldiers. He manages to outwit the army psychiatrists and is rejected by the Army.

Malcolm's younger brother, Reginald, who joined the merchant marines, begins visiting Malcolm. Malcolm introduces him to the exciting musical world of New York, and to such music legends as Billie Holiday and Lionel Hampton. Reginald starts dating a black waitress, who completely pampers him. He and Malcolm become close friends.

Meanwhile, racial tension in Harlem is steadily increasing. Thus, when word gets out that white policemen have shot a black soldier in a Harlem hotel, angry Harlem residents riot and loot neighborhood businesses. After the riot, white people are more fearful and stop visiting Harlem. Consequently, Harlem's hustlers and prostitutes, whose main source of income was white people's money, are forced to find legitimate work.

In 1945, Malcolm begins committing armed robberies with Sammy the Pimp. When Malcolm becomes a numbers runner and pimp, he ventures outside of Harlem. Soon, he gets a job working for Hymie, transporting bootleg liquor from Long Island to New York bars. Hymie mysteriously disappears after a rumor spreads that he is a government informant.

As Chapter 7 concludes, Malcolm's own life has been threatened. He expresses his deep gratitude to God for having helped him survive this decadent life of crime.

Analysis

The reader is overwhelmed by Malcolm's detailed and compelling account of his drug use, pimping, hustling, and armed robbery activities. The use of similes and metaphors helps one easily visualize the people and events. When Malcolm describes the pimp,

"Cadillac" Drake, he notes, "He was shiny baldheaded, built like a football."

Interestingly, it is during this period in his life that Malcolm develops an obsession with going to the movies. The reader can conjecture that movies are Malcolm's only means of escape from his depraved existence.

Feeling frustrated and trapped by his circumstances, Malcolm uses animal imagery to describe himself. He says, "When you become an animal, a vulture, in the ghetto, as I had become, you enter a world of animals and vultures. It becomes truly survival of only the fittest." The reader strongly empathizes with Malcolm as he compares himself to a vulture. Malcolm's sense of extreme degradation and helplessness is a recurring theme during this period of his life.

Study Questions

1. How did the burglar, "Jumpsteady," get his name?

2. Why is Malcolm fired from Small's Paradise?

3. How old is Malcolm when he becomes a drug peddler?

4. Why is Malcolm wary of taking Sophia out to Roxbury clubs?

5. Why does Malcolm begin traveling on railroad lines?

6. What caused the 1945 riot in Harlem?

7. What is West Indian Archie's unique ability?

8. Why does Malcolm visit his brother, Philbert, in Michigan?

9. Who is Branch Rickey? Why are people in Harlem excited about Rickey's recent decision?

10. What is Malcolm's main job when he works for Hymie?

Answers

1. "Jumpsteady" gets his name from his days as a burglar when he jumped from the rooftops of buildings and maneuvered along window ledges.

2. Malcolm is fired from Small's Paradise because, one day, while at work, he gives an undercover policeman the telephone number of a prostitute.

3. Malcolm becomes a drug peddler when he is 17 years old.

4. Malcolm is wary of taking Sophia out to Roxbury clubs because "the Boston cops used the war as an excuse to harass interracial couples, stopping them and grilling the Negro about his draft status."

5. Malcolm begins traveling on the railroad lines because it is a safe way for him to sell marijuana to touring musicians.

6. In 1945, white merchants in Harlem refused to hire black people to work in their stores. Thousands of angry black people began to riot in retaliation.

7. West Indian Archie's unique ability is that he has a photographic memory.

8. Malcolm visits his brother, Philbert, because Malcolm matched the description of the man who had robbed a Harlem bar. He leaves New York, temporarily, until the real thief is caught.

9. Branch Rickey is the owner of the Brooklyn Dodgers. In 1945, he signs the black baseball player, Jackie Robinson, to play in major league baseball.

10. Malcolm transports bootleg liquor from Long Island to New York bars.

Suggested Essay Topics

1. In describing the racism that black people experienced, Malcolm says, "All of us . . . were . . . black victims of the white man's American social system." Explain how the racial prejudice of the times had a negative impact on Malcolm.

2. Although Malcolm and his younger brother, Reginald, have very different personalities, the two become very close friends. Compare and contrast these two men.

Chapter 8: Trapped
Chapter 9: Caught

New People:

Sophia's 17-year old sister: *dates Shorty*

John Hughes: *owns a gambling house in Boston*

Rudy: *a friend of Shorty's and a member of Malcolm's burglary ring*

Sophia's husband: *goes looking for Malcolm when he finds out Sophia has been seeing him*

Sophia's husband's friend: *takes Sophia and her sister out to dinner*

Detective Slack: *police detective investigating Malcolm*

Detective Turner: *police detective investigating Malcolm*

Summary

Malcolm moves back to Boston after West Indian Archie, who wrongfully believes Malcolm has stolen money from him, threatens to kill him. Malcolm lives with his longtime friend, Shorty, and continues his reckless drug use and gambling. Ella is shocked by Malcolm's corrupt behavior. Shorty begins dating Sophia's 17-year old sister, who remains unnamed throughout the autobiography.

Malcolm organizes a burglary ring with Shorty, Sophia, Sophia's sister, and Rudy. The two women are used to scout out wealthy white neighborhoods, Malcolm and Shorty rob houses, and Rudy serves as the driver of the getaway car. They find a fence who purchases and resells the stolen articles. The burglary ring is successful for nearly one year.

One day, however, Malcolm goes to a jewelry shop to pick up a stolen watch that he had brought in for repair. He had decided to keep this expensive watch for himself and, unbeknownst to him, local jewelers have been on the lookout for stolen merchandise. Malcolm is arrested. Shorty and the two women are also arrested; Rudy manages to escape.

The racist social workers and the court-appointed lawyer assigned to the case think that Malcolm and Shorty have committed a gravely serious offense. To them, the crime of robbery was secondary; Malcolm and his companions have committed a more serious crime. As Malcolm explains, "Nobody wanted to know anything at all about the robberies. All they could see was that we had taken the white man's woman."

Analysis

Malcolm continues to use many stylistic devices to describe his moral and physical decline. He reminisces, "Looking back, I think I really was at least slightly out of my mind. I viewed narcotics as most people regard food. I wore my guns as today I wear my neckties. Deep down, I actually believed that after living as fully as humanly possible, one should then die violently...I think I deliberately invited death in many, sometimes insane ways." The reader notes that here is one of several occasions in the autobiography where Malcolm, quite prophetically, predicts his own death.

Later on, after challenging Detective Turner to a gunfight in a bar, Malcolm writes, "I had gotten to the point where I was walking on my own coffin." The reader is both horrified and profoundly moved by his gripping, fatalistic attitude about his life.

It has always been extremely important to Malcolm to gain the respect and admiration of the people around him. As a result, when the members of his burglary ring meet for the first time, Malcolm is compelled to act (seemingly) recklessly by playing a game of Russian roulette. He falsely appears to place his own life in jeopardy. (In the *Autobiography*'s Epilogue, Alex Haley writes that Malcolm admitted to him that this action was a ruse. Malcolm's gun actually contained no bullets when he put the muzzle to his head and pulled the trigger!) Not only does Malcolm gain their utmost respect, but, he concludes, "They thought I was crazy. They were afraid of me."

Malcolm continues to enjoy deceiving white people. He admits, "I knew that the white man is rare who will ever consider that a Negro can outsmart him." On one occasion, when he and the other members of his burglary ring are driving away from a heist, they spot a police car following them. To allay any suspicions that the police officers may have, Malcolm gets out of the car, flags the

officers down, and proceeds to ask them directions. The officers give him directions and drive away, without the slightest misgivings.

At the conclusion of Chapter 9, Malcolm explains his reasons for writing his autobiography. He says, "To understand . . . any person, his whole life, from birth, must be reviewed. All of our experiences fuse into our personality. Everything that happened to us is an ingredient . . . the full story is the best way that I know to have it seen, and understood, that I had sunk to the very bottom of the American white man's society when—soon now, in prison—I found Allah and the religion of Islam and it completely transformed my life."

The reader recognizes that Malcolm's "nightmare," which began in early childhood and continued into his teenage and early adult years, has ended; redemption and salvation are forthcoming.

Study Questions

1. What is Billie Holiday's nickname?

2. Why does Shorty come to New York?

3. Why is Ella shocked when she sees Malcolm after he has moved back to Boston?

4. How much money does Malcolm's cocaine habit cost him daily?

5. What is a "finder"?

6. Why does Malcolm decide to include white girls in his burglary operation?

7. Why does Malcolm often go to the Savoy nightclub after burglarizing homes?

8. How does Sophia's husband find out about her relationship with Malcolm?

9. At the time Malcolm is arrested, who is at his apartment?

10. What is the attitude of Malcolm's lawyer toward his arrest?

Answers

1. Billie Holiday's nickname is Lady Day.

2. Shorty comes to New York after receiving a phone call from Sammy, telling him that Malcolm needs his help.

3. Ella is shocked when she sees Malcolm because she thinks he has become an atheist; he is uncouth and full of profanity.

4. Malcolm's cocaine habit costs him $20 daily.

5. A "finder" is a person who locates wealthy homes to rob.

6. Malcolm decides to include white girls in his burglary operation for two reasons. First, he thinks white women would be good "finders." Second, they would not "stick out like sore thumbs" in white residential areas.

7. Malcolm goes to the Savoy after burglarizing homes because, if it were ever necessary, the bar patrons could testify that he had been at the bar at the time a burglary was committed.

8. Sophia's husband's friend tells her husband about Sophia's relationship with Malcolm.

9. When Malcolm is arrested, Sophia's husband is at his apartment.

10. Malcolm's lawyer is angry about Malcolm's involvement with white women.

Suggested Essay Topics

1. As Malcolm looks back on his life, he admits that he "deliberately invited death" many times. Give two examples that justify this statement.

2. Malcolm is fortunate to have several people in his life who help him during times of crises. Name two of these people. How do they offer Malcolm guidance and support?

Chapter 10: Satan

New People:

Bimbi: *Malcolm's fellow inmate in Charlestown State Prison*

John: *Malcolm's fellow inmate in Norfolk Prison Colony*

The Honorable Elijah Muhammad: *the leader of the Nation of Islam*

"Mr. Yacub": *according to the teachings of Elijah Muhammad, he created the white race 6,600 years ago*

Master W.D. Fard: *a half-black, half-white man who gave Elijah Muhammad Allah's message and divine guidance*

Summary

In 1946, Malcolm is sentenced to ten years in prison. He is sent to the dilapidated Charlestown State Prison with his friend Shorty, who has been given an eight-to-ten year sentence. Malcolm's wild atheistic rantings in prison earn him the nickname "Satan." He meets Bimbi and develops enormous respect for this articulate, well-read black man. With Bimbi's encouragement, Malcolm enrolls in prison correspondence courses.

Meanwhile, Malcolm's brothers and sisters have converted to the religion of Islam and want their brother to convert as well. His brother, Reginald, advises him in a letter to stop eating pork and smoking cigarettes. Malcolm thinks that Reginald's instructions have some hidden meaning. He thinks that by following his brother's advice, he would begin experiencing physical problems and, thus, be released from prison early. Malcolm gives up eating pork and smoking cigarettes with surprisingly little difficulty.

Thanks to Ella's efforts, Malcolm is transferred to the Norfolk (Massachusetts) Prison Colony, an experimental rehabilitation jail, in 1948. The Colony has a wide variety of educational programs and an extensive library collection.

Reginald visits Malcolm and explains that followers of the Honorable Elijah Muhammad abstain from cigarettes, pork, narcotics,

and liquor. Muhammad, he says, is the black leader of the Nation of Islam and the "Messenger of Allah [God]." Muhammad preaches that the black man has been "brainwashed for hundreds of years" by "the devil white men." Reginald cites numerous examples of the white man's oppression and exploitation of black people throughout the centuries—such as the evils of black slavery, and the "whitened" history books that fail to mention the past cultures and traditions of African-American people. Malcolm's sister, Hilda, also visits and tells him more about Muhammad's teachings.

Analysis

The theme of transformation is very evident in this chapter. Significantly, as the chapter opens, the reader learns that Malcolm has been nicknamed "Satan." Later, "Satan" is said to be, ironically, the white man, who, according to Muhammad's teachings, has oppressed and enslaved black people for centuries.

The description of black people's history of suffering and oppression at the hands of white people is quite vivid and has a profound effect on Malcolm. Reginald tells him, "You have been a victim of the evil of the devil white man ever since he murdered and raped and stole you from your native land in the seeds of your forefathers." Malcolm's recollection of his own interactions with white people serve to validate Muhammad's theories.

Malcolm explains his first reaction to Muhammad's ideas: "Every instinct of the ghetto jungle streets, every hustling fox and criminal wolf instinct in me, which would have scoffed at and rejected anything else, was struck dumb. It was as though all of that life merely was back there, without any remaining effect, or influence."

Malcolm expresses his willingness to accept Muhammad's ideas, saying, "I have since learned—helping me to understand what then began to happen within me—that the truth can be quickly received, or received at all, only by the sinner who knows and admits that he is guilty of having sinned much....The very enormity of my previous life's guilt prepared me to accept the truth."

However, as the chapter ends, Malcolm acknowledges, in retrospect, that Muhammad was a "religious faker" who misled African–Americans. For the reader, this statement represents a clear foreshadowing of Malcolm's future conflict with Muhammad.

Study Questions

1. Where were Sophia and her sister sent?

2. When was the Charlestown prison built?

3. Who is Malcolm's first visitor in prison?

4. What subjects does Malcolm study in his correspondence courses?

5. What is the reaction of the other inmates to Malcolm's refusal to eat pork?

6. How many inmates does the Norfolk Prison Colony have?

7. Where was Elijah Muhammad born?

8. Where does Elijah Muhammad stay when he visits Detroit?

9. According to Elijah Muhammad's teachings, from what tribe do America's blacks descend?

10. Who was Master W.D. Fard?

Answers

1. Sophia and her sister were sent to the Women's Reformatory at Framingham, Massachusetts.

2. Charlestown State Prison was built in 1805.

3. Ella was Malcolm's first visitor in prison.

4. Malcolm studies grammar and Latin.

5. The other inmates are surprised at Malcolm's refusal to eat pork.

6. The Norfolk Prison Colony has 1200 inmates.

7. Elijah Muhammad was born on a farm in Georgia.

8. Elijah Muhammad stays at the house of Wilfred, Malcolm's brother.

9. America's blacks descend from the strong black tribe of Shabazz.

10. Master W.D. Fard was considered a god, and gave Elijah Muhammad Allah's message.

Suggested Essay Topics

1. All of Malcolm's brothers and sisters are eager to convert Malcolm. Reginald proves to be the most persuasive. Why is he successful in converting Malcolm?

2. Upon learning the history of black people's oppression, Malcolm says, "the truth . . . was like a blinding light." Explain this simile.

Chapter 11: Saved
Chapter 12: Savior

New People:

Lemuel Hassan: *minister of Detroit's Temple Number One*

Sister Clara Muhammad: *Elijah Muhammad's wife*

Mother Marie: *Elijah Muhammad's mother*

Summary

In Norfolk Prison Colony, Malcolm devotes himself to studying the teachings of Muhammad. In addition, he reads the classics, and studies philosophy, science, and world history. Each day, he writes a letter to Muhammad, professing his devotion to the Nation of Islam. He writes letters to his former friends and acquaintances from his hustling days, telling them about his newfound religion. He writes letters, protesting "how the white man's society was responsible for the black man's condition in this wilderness of North America," to various politicians—the Mayor of Boston, the Governor, and to Harry S. Truman, the President of the United States!

He is shocked and dismayed when he discovers that Reginald, for whom he has had so much respect, has been suspended from the Nation of Islam because of Reginald's illicit relationship with the secretary of the Nation of Islam's New York Temple.

Malcolm is transferred back to the Charlestown Prison, ostensibly because he refused to take an inoculation. Malcolm is certain, however, that the real reason for the transfer is his affiliation and conversion to the religion of Islam.

Upon his release from prison in 1952, Malcolm returns to Detroit to continue his Islamic studies. He lives with Wilfred and his family, and works as a salesman in a furniture store managed by Wilfred.

Malcolm yearns to prove his commitment to The Nation of Islam. He is thrilled when he meets Elijah Muhammad for the first time at a Muslim rally in Chicago in 1952. In an effort to increase Nation of Islam membership, Malcolm initiates a recruitment drive, and tirelessly visits Detroit's bars, poolrooms, and streets. The membership of Detroit's Temple One nearly triples.

Malcolm changes his last name from "Little" to "X," to symbolize the long-lost African name that he never knew. With encouragement from Minister Lemuel Hassan, Malcolm begins preaching in temple, and electrifies his audience. He continues working in various factories while spreading the teachings of Muhammad.

One day, an F.B.I. agent visits Malcolm at work to find out why he has not registered for the Korean War draft. Malcolm explains that, as a former prison convict, he did not think he would be accepted into the army. Actually, Malcolm knows that ex-convicts can serve in the army; he was attempting to outwit the agent. When Malcolm goes to the draft board to register, he is more forthright about his reasons for not registering earlier. He explains that he is "a conscientious objector . . . I told them that when the white man asked me to go off somewhere and fight and maybe die to preserve the way the white man treated the black man in America, then my conscience made me object." He is given a deferment.

Analysis

In Chapters 11 and 12, Malcolm continues to read and educate himself about black people's long and tragic history in America. He learns more and more about the teachings of Muhammad. The reader sees Malcolm's transformation as a process of spiritual and intellectual growth. In this stage of his life, Malcolm is using those skills that made him a successful street hustler—his eloquence and intuition—to become a successful, well-respected minister for the Nation of Islam.

The language that Malcolm uses to stir up his temple audience is provocative and evokes anger. He presents a scathing indictment of white people, declaring, "That rapist slavemaster who emasculated the black man . . . with threats, with fear . . . until even today the black man lives with fear of the white man in his heart! Lives even today under the heel of the white man!"

In contrast, the language Malcolm uses in these chapters to cite the historical references of black people's mistreatment by white people is scholarly and erudite. He chronicles the history of other non-white ethnic groups—Indians and Chinese people, for example—and describes the prejudices they have encountered throughout the centuries, as well.

Referring to the present time (when he wrote his autobiography in the early 1960s), Malcolm is still convinced that the plight of black people in the United States today is far worse than that of other non-white people in the world. He writes, "The American black man is the world's most shameful case of minority oppression."

At the conclusion of Chapter 12, the reader is again forewarned of Malcolm's impending conflict. He writes, "In the years to come, I was going to have to face a psychological and spiritual crisis."

Study Questions

1. Who was Nat Turner?

2. In addition to the United States, Malcolm names two countries whose non-white citizens have suffered as a result of white people. Name these countries.

3. What does the five-pointed Islamic star stand for?

4. Why does Malcolm begin to wear glasses?

5. What did Shorty do while he was in prison?

6. What does Malcolm buy when he is released from prison?

7. What are Elijah Muhammad's recommendations to Malcolm about how to increase membership in the Nation of Islam?

8. Malcolm compares his visits with Elijah Muhammad with "Socrates on the steps of the Athens market place." Explain the analogy.

9. Why was Elijah Muhammad forced to quit school?

10. How many children do Elijah Muhammad and his wife have?

Answers

1. Nat Turner was a slave preacher. In 1831, he led a slave insurrection, killing 57 white people. He was caught and hanged for the murders two months later.

2. India and China are the two countries Malcolm names.

3. The five-pointed Islamic star stands for justice and the five senses of man.

4. Malcolm begins wearing glasses because he developed an astigmatism in prison from reading in the dark.

5. Shorty studied and wrote musical compositions while he was in prison.

6. Malcolm buys a better-looking pair of glasses, a suitcase, and a wristwatch when he is released from prison.

7. Elijah Muhammad recommends that Malcolm "Go after the young people. Once you get them, the older ones will follow through shame."

8. Malcolm and Elijah drove along the streets of Chicago, visiting Muslim-owned grocery stores. Muhammad would spread the teachings of the Nation of Islam, as Socrates would spread his wisdom to his students.

9. Elijah Muhammad quit school because his family was very poor and he had to start working.

10. Elijah Muhammad and his wife have eight children.

Chapter 13: Minister Malcolm X

New People:

Brother Lloyd X: *a Muslim follower in Boston, Massachusetts*

Brother Osborne: *a Muslim follower in Springfield, Massachusetts*

Brother James X: *a Muslim follower in Atlanta, Georgia*

Sister Betty X: *Malcolm's wife*

Brother John Ali and his wife: *a couple who share a house with Malcolm and his wife in Queens, New York*

Various Brothers and Sisters: *Muslim followers*

Summary
Malcolm quits his factory job to work fulltime spreading Elijah Muhammad's teachings. He travels all along the East Coast, opening numerous Muslim temples. He visits several of his old friends in Boston, including Shorty and West Indian Archie. In 1958, he marries Betty X.

Malcolm is appointed minister of Temple Seven in New York City's Harlem, and he and Betty move to Queens, New York. Malcolm is disgusted and angered when two Muslim brothers become victims of police brutality in Harlem. Malcolm effectively

handles the potentially explosive situation.

Analysis

Malcolm is assimilating extraordinarily well in his new life, earning the respect of both Elijah Muhammad and his peers. Malcolm's current lifestyle bears no resemblance to his days of street hustling and thievery. This contrast is further evidenced when Malcolm visits Boston and observes the marked decline of his old friends.

As the chapter concludes, Malcolm demonstrates his growing maturity and evolution. Two Muslim men have been hit in the head with nightsticks by white policemen, who were breaking up a street scuffle. Malcolm immediately assumes control of this potentially explosive situation. He leads a large group of Muslims on a peaceful march to Harlem Hospital, where the injured men are being treated. Malcolm writes, "Harlem's black people...never had seen any organization of black men take a firm stand as we were."

Study Questions

1. How long does it take Ella to decide to convert to Islam?

2. What does Shorty do for a living?

3. What is the City of Brotherly Love?

4. What is the Muslims' strict moral code?

5. When Malcolm conducts a funeral service, he explains that no tears are shed, and there are no flowers, singing, or organ-playing. What explanation does he offer for this?

6. What is the Muslim Temple's Unity Night?

7. Describe the problem Betty X has with her foster parents.

8. Where do Malcolm and Betty get married?

9. How many children do Malcolm and Betty have? Name them.

10. What is the outcome of Brother Hinton's injuries?

Answers

1. It takes Ella five years to decide to convert to Islam.

2. Shorty has a little band in Boston.

3. The City of Brotherly Love is Philadelphia.

4. The Muslims' strict moral code forbids fornication, pork, to-bacco, alcohol, and narcotics. Dancing, attending movies or sports games, taking long vacations, lying, stealing, and in-subordination to civil authority are also forbidden. Domestic quarreling and discourtesy—especially to women—are not allowed.

5. Malcolm explains that the reason there are no tears, flowers, or music during a funeral service is because these were things that people gave to the deceased when he was alive. Now, there is no need for these things, since the deceased is not aware of anything. The money that would be spent for these items should go to the family, instead.

6. The Muslims' Unity Night, on Tuesday nights, is an opportunity for Muslim brothers and sisters to enjoy each other's company and have refreshments.

7. Betty X's foster parents were against her association with the Muslims, and threatened to stop financing her nursing education.

8. Malcolm and Betty get married in Lansing, Michigan.

9. Malcolm and Betty have four daughters—Attilah, Qubilah, Ilyasah, and Amilah.

10. As a result of his injuries, Brother Hinton has a steel plate in his skull. In addition, he sues the police and is awarded $70,000.

Suggested Essay Topics

1. What are Malcolm's attitudes toward women before he meets Betty?

2. Malcolm describes a situation of police brutality that occurs in Harlem. Explain the significance of Malcolm's skillful handling of the situation.

Chapter 14: Black Muslims

New People:

Louis Lomax: *black journalist who profiles the Nation of Islam in a television documentary*

Professor C. Eric Lincoln: *black scholar who writes a book about the Nation of Islam*

James Hicks: *editor of the* Amsterdam News, *a Harlem newspaper*

Summary

The Nation of Islam movement is gaining national, as well as international, prominence. In 1959, two newspapers serving black communities, Harlem's *Amsterdam News* and Los Angeles' *Herald Dispatch*, begin carrying regular columns written by Malcolm and Elijah Muhammad about the Nation of Islam. Malcolm founds a newspaper, *Muhammad Speaks*, and visits Africa to spread Elijah Muhammad's teachings.

However, after a television documentary profiles the Nation of Islam's ideology about the "devil white man," public condemnation is swift. Newspapers denounce the movement's "hate-messengers" and "black supremacists." Malcolm appears on several radio and television programs to defend the Nation of Islam. He appears at mass rallies as Elijah Muhammad's right-hand man.

Analysis

The fiery speeches of Malcolm and Elijah Muhammad evoke a wide range of audience emotions—from shock and rage to admiration and self-pride. Their speeches are filled with emotionally charged words and images, meant to arouse and incite listeners. Calling white people "oppressors," Elijah Muhammad declares, "A thousand ways every day, the white man is telling you 'You can't live here. You can't enter here'...You have tilled his fields! Cooked his food! Washed his clothes! . . . So let us, the black people, *separate* ourselves from this white man slavemaster."

Malcolm continues to worship Muhammad, who is a father-figure to him. As the chapter concludes, Muhammad advises Malcolm, "Brother Malcolm, I want you to become well known....You will grow to be hated when you become well known. Because usually people get jealous of public figures." Malcolm comments, in retrospect, on this remark, saying, "Nothing that Mr. Muhammad ever said to me was more prophetic." Once again, Malcolm is forewarning the reader about a future conflict between the two men.

Study Questions

1. As Muhammad's emissary, what African countries does Malcolm visit in 1959?

2. What is the name of the television documentary that profiles the Nation of Islam?

3. What "demagogues" does Malcolm compare Muhammad to? Name three.

4. What national magazines run stories about the Nation of Islam?

5. Who coined the name "Black Muslims"?

6. According to Malcolm, what do America's law enforcement agencies do to keep track of the Nation of Islam?

7. Aside from health concerns, why is Malcolm so adamantly against smoking?

8. What will the proposed Islamic Center in Chicago contain?

9. What type of health problems does Muhammad have?

10. Where does Muhammad live most of the year as a result of his health problems?

Answers

1. Malcolm visits Egypt, Arabia, the Sudan, Nigeria, and Ghana as Muhammad's emissary.

2. The name of the television program is "The Hate That Hate Produced."

3. Malcolm compares Muhammad to "demagogues" like Socrates, Jesus Christ, Gandhi, Galileo, and Martin Luther.

4. *Life, Look, Newsweek, Time,* and *Reader's Digest* run stories about the Nation of Islam.

5. The name "Black Muslims" comes from the title of Professor Lincoln's book, "The Black Muslims in America."

6. According to Malcolm, law enforcement agents watch Muslims, tap their telephones, and use black agents to infiltrate the Nation of Islam.

7. Malcolm is adamantly against smoking because he is against supporting the white-controlled government, which receives the tobacco industry's billions of dollars in tax revenues.

8. The proposed Islamic Center will contain a beautiful mosque, school, library, hospital, and a museum, and will document black history.

9. Muhammad has a bronchial asthmatic condition.

10. Muhammad lives in the dry climate of Phoenix, Arizona because of his health problems.

Suggested Essay Topics

1. Malcolm teaches that the only solution for black people in America is complete "separation" from white people. He makes a distinction between "separation" and "segregation." Explain the differences between the two terms.

2. What is the public's reaction to the ideology of the Nation of Islam? In your opinion, is their reaction justified? Explain.

Chapter 15: Icarus

Summary

Malcolm becomes a much sought-after speaker on the lecture circuit. He is an incredibly powerful and charismatic speaker, preaching about past and current injustices and the atrocities that have been committed by white men against black people.

Analysis

The reader is deeply affected by Malcolm's use of intensely graphic details to describe white people's inhumanity toward non-white people throughout history. For example, he cites America's bombings of Hiroshima and Nagasaki during World War II, noting that America chose to drop the atomic bomb on its non-white, Japanese enemy rather than on its white, Nazi German enemy. He speaks of the injustice of the internment camps that America used to imprison Japanese-American citizens during World War II. He asks, "What about the one hundred thousand loyal naturalized and native-born Japanese American citizens who were herded into camps, behind barbed wire?"

To convince his audience of the overwhelming need for black separatism, he draws an analogy between Jewish people's desire to set up a homeland in Israel, and the Nation of Islam's desire to live apart from white people.

At the chapter's conclusion, Malcolm experiences a shocking discovery when he appears at Boston's Harvard Law School Forum as a guest speaker. He realizes that his old burglary gang's hideout is right down the street. He thinks, "Scenes from my once depraved life lashed through my mind. Living like an animal; thinking like an animal!"

Study Questions

1. Who was Rosa Parks?

2. Why does Malcolm say it is "ridiculous" for Northern white and black Freedom Riders to demonstrate in the South?

3. What ethnic or religious groups does Malcolm use as examples of the problems with "assimilation"?

4. Who originally suggested having a March on Washington?

5. What song was sung during the 1963 civil rights' March on Washington?

6. What two publications increased Malcolm's popularity?

7. What situation does Malcolm cite to prove that Jewish people exploit black people?

8. Who does a *New York Times* poll indicate to be "the second most sought after" speaker at colleges and universities?

9. Who are the three most important prophets of the religion of Islam?

10. Malcolm believes that if he had not converted to the religion of Islam, his life would have been drastically different. What does he think he would have done?

Answers

1. Rosa Parks was an African-American resident of Montgomery, Alabama. In 1955, she refused to give up her seat on a bus to a white person. Her action touched off a local boycott that eventually desegregated Montgomery's buses, and also inspired more people to join the civil rights movement.

2. Malcolm says it is "ridiculous" for Northerners to go to the South to demonstrate since black people have severe social and economic problems in the North.

3. The Irish, English, French Canadians, Canadians, Jewish people, and the Germans all have had problems with assimilation.

4. A. Philip Randolph originally suggested having the March on Washington.

5. "We Shall Overcome" was sung during the March on Washington.

6. Lincoln's book, *The Black Muslims in America,* and an inter-

view with Malcolm that was printed in *Playboy* magazine, increased his popularity.

7. Malcolm cites the Jewish-owned businesses that, he claims, are in every black ghetto. He says these businesses help to maintain black poverty.

8. The poll indicates that Malcolm X is "the second most sought after" speaker at colleges and universities.

9. The three most important prophets are Jesus Christ, Mohammad, and Moses.

10. Malcolm believes he would have been dead, a convict, or a patient in an insane asylum.

Suggested Essay Topics

1. Malcolm makes a clear distinction between the white Southerner and the Northern white "liberal." From Malcolm's viewpoint, how do white Americans from these two geographical areas differ?

2. Who was Icarus? Why does Malcolm compare himself to Icarus?

Chapter 16: Out

New People:

Dr. Leona A. Turner: *Malcolm's family doctor*

Cassius Clay: *famous Muslim heavyweight boxer*

Sonny Liston: *famous heavyweight boxer who fights Cassius Clay*

Floyd Patterson: *famous heavyweight boxer who fights Cassius Clay*

Summary

Thanks to Malcolm's tenacity and dedication to the Nation of Islam, more than 100 mosques opened throughout the United

States by 1961. Although his commitment to the movement remains unswerving, he is convinced that "our Nation of Islam could
be an even greater force in the American black man's overall
struggle—if we engaged in more action."

Meanwhile, Malcolm has become aware of the fact that negative remarks were being made about him by people within the
Nation of Islam. They were saying, for example, that Malcolm likes
being a "coast-to-coast Mr. Big Shot." Remembering Elijah
Mohammad's prediction about people's envy and jealousy toward
public figures, Malcolm is not angry or upset by these comments.
Soon, he starts to notice that he is receiving less coverage in the
Nation of Islam's newspaper, *Muhammad Speaks.* Malcolm, again,
refuses to allow this to bother him, because he considers resentful
feelings to be a sign of weakness. Eventually, however, in 1963,
Malcolm is so distressed by Muslims' reactions to him that, attempting to escape the limelight, he begins to turn down journalists' requests for interviews.

During this time, rumors have begun to circulate about Elijah
Muhammad's allegedly adulterous affairs. In 1963, America's mass
media reports these allegations, and Malcolm is horrified. The
Nation of Islam's strict moral code forbids such behavior. In fact,
Malcolm's own brother, Reginald, was expelled from the Nation
several years earlier as a result of a similar type of moral misconduct.

On November 22, 1963, President John F. Kennedy is assassinated in Dallas, Texas. Malcolm believes the President's assassination demonstrates that "the hate in white men had not stopped
with the killing of defenseless people, but that hate, allowed to
spread unchecked, finally had struck down this country's Chief of
State." When asked his opinion about this tragedy, Malcolm replies
that it is a case of "the chickens coming home to roost." Taken out
of context, this remark seems disrespectful and brash to people.

In an effort to disassociate Muslims from Malcolm's statement,
Elijah Muhammad silences him for 90 days. Malcolm is deeply
troubled and at the same time—given the reaction of Muslims to
him in recent years—suspicious of Muhammad's denouncement.
He visits his family doctor, and she advises him to get more rest.
Malcolm and Betty, along with their three daughters, go on their

Scales of Justice

first vacation since their marriage. In honor of Malcolm and Betty's sixth anniversary, their friend, Cassius Clay, takes them to Miami. Malcolm attends the championship boxing match between the underdog Clay, a Muslim, and Sonny Liston, a Christian. Clay triumphs.

Back in New York, Malcolm announces plans to create an organization which would "help to challenge the American black man to gain his human rights, and to cure his mental, spiritual, economic, and political sicknesses. . . . It would embrace all faiths of black men, and it would carry into practice what the Nation of Islam had only preached." People are enthusiastic about Malcolm's new mosque, called Muslim Mosque, Inc.

To prepare himself for this enormous commitment, Malcolm decides to make a pilgrimage to the holy city of Mecca, in Saudi Arabia, which is the birthplace of Muhammad, who was an Arab prophet and the founder of Islam in the seventh century.

Analysis

The conflict detailed in this chapter is between Malcolm and Elijah Muhammad's Nation of Islam. Although Malcolm has alluded to this conflict in previous chapters, Muhammad's total repudiation of Malcolm takes the reader by surprise.

As the title indicates, the chapter describes how Malcolm is kicked "out" of the Nation of Islam. The reader empathizes with Malcolm, and recognizes that these events are a part of the process of his evolution. The reader learns that Malcolm has become somewhat disillusioned with the Nation of Islam movement because of its "all talk, no action," or "non-engagement" policy in response to the black man's struggle for equal rights. Then, there is the Muslim followers' growing negativity toward him, his exclusion from coverage in the Nation's newspaper, and, finally, Malcolm's torment when he learns about Elijah Muhammad's betrayal of the Muslims' strict moral code.

The ultimate blow to Malcolm comes when he is "silenced" by Elijah Muhammad because of his comments regarding the assassination of President John Kennedy.

Malcolm's language in this chapter lacks the descriptive similes and metaphors used in previous chapters. His language is quite factual and journalistic, particularly toward the end of the chapter, when he has recognized Muhammad's betrayal and is clearly focusing on ways to remedy the situation.

The chapter concludes on a positive note, as Malcolm announces the formation of a new organization and his intentions to make a pilgrimage to Mecca. His organization will be substantially different from the Nation of Islam's "talk only" policy. Malcolm asserts that the strength of "a ten-million black vote bloc could be the deciding balance of power in American politics. . . . The polls are one place where every black man could fight the black man's cause with dignity, and with the power and the tools that the white man understands, and respects, and fears, and cooperates with." Malcolm sums up, "It will be the working base for an action program designed to eliminate the political oppression, the economic exploitation, and the social degradation suffered daily by twenty-two million Afro-Americans."

Study Questions

1. Why does Betty have an argument with Malcolm?

2. In 1962, Malcolm refers to a "climate of hate" in the United States. What specific incidents is he speaking about?

3. Where do Malcolm and Muhammad make their last public appearance together?

4. How did Elijah Muhammad allegedly betray the Nation of Islam's strict moral code?

5. What does Malcolm do to find out the truth about Elijah Muhammad's alleged misconduct?

6. What directives are Muslim ministers given in response to the assassination of President John Kennedy?

7. How does Malcolm respond when asked his opinion about President Kennedy's assassination?

8. Whom does Malcolm depend on for spiritual strength during his suspension from the Nation of Islam?

9. How does Malcolm think black people can gain political influence?

10. Who helps Malcolm finance his pilgrimage to Mecca?

Answers

1. Betty has an argument with Malcolm because she wants him to consider his family more and put away money for the future.

2. The specific incidents that Malcolm refers to are the assassination of N.A.A.C.P. (National Association for the Advancement of Colored People) Field Secretary Medgar Evers in Mississippi, and the bombing of a black Christian church that killed four young black girls.

3. Malcolm and Elijah Muhammad made their last public appearance together at a rally in Philadelphia.

4. Elijah Muhammad allegedly betrayed the Nation of Islam's strict moral code by committing adultery with two of his secretaries.

5. To find out the truth about Elijah Muhammad's alleged misconduct, Malcolm looks up and talks with three of Muhammad's former secretaries.

6. Muslim ministers were given the directive to make no remarks concerning the assassination of President Kennedy. They were told that if they were pressed for an answer, to respond by saying, "No comment."

7. Malcolm responds that he saw the assassination as a case of "the chickens coming home to roost."

8. Malcolm depends on Betty for spiritual strength during his suspension.

9. Malcolm thinks black people can gain political influence by creating a black voting bloc, which would contain ten million voting black citizens.

10. Ella helps Malcolm finance his pilgrimage to Mecca.

Suggested Essay Topics

1. Malcolm mentions the "economic exploitation suffered daily by black people," and cites examples to prove this statement. What specific examples does he cite?

2. Compare and contrast the philosophies of Malcolm's new organization, the Muslim Mosque, Inc. and Elijah Muhammad's Nation of Islam.

Chapter 17: Mecca

New People:

Wallace Muhammad: *Elijah Muhammad's son and Malcolm's friend*

Dr. Mahmoud Youssef Shawarbi: *a Muslim lecturer, writer, professor, United Nations advisor, and close advisor to Prince Faisal, who helps Malcolm make his pilgrimage to Mecca*

Prince Faisal: *the ruler of Saudi Arabia*

Abd ir-Rahman Azzam: *author of* The Eternal Message of Muhammad, *who lives in Jedda*

Muhammad Shawarbi: s*on of Dr. Shawarbi; a student at Cairo University*

Dr. Omar Azzam: *son of Mr. Azzam, and a Swiss-trained engineer who lives in Jedda*

Muhammad, the Mutawaf: a *young man who serves as a guide to Malcolm on his pilgrimage to Mecca*

Hussein Amiri, the Grand Mufti of Jerusalem: *a Muslim leader*

Sheikh Muhammad Harkon: *judge of the Muslim High Court*

Summary

Malcolm makes plans for his pilgrimage to the Holy City of Mecca. On his way to Mecca, his plane stops in Frankfurt, Germany and Cairo, Egypt. There, he goes sightseeing, meeting very friendly and hospitable people.

Upon his arrival in Jedda, an ancient seaport town in Saudi Arabia, Malcolm is temporarily delayed at the airport. He learns that, prior to his pilgrimage, he must first appear before "the Muslim high court which examined all possibly non-authentic converts to the Islamic religion seeking to enter Mecca."

Bewildered and unable to communicate with the Arabic-speaking people he meets at the airport, Malcolm contacts Dr. Assam. Dr. Assam and his family provide him with food and lodging. The high court approves Malcolm's pilgrimage to Mecca.

Along his pilgrimage, Malcolm encounters thousands of people of various racial and ethnic backgrounds. He is amazed by the true sense of "brotherhood" practiced by all of these people, "irrespective of color." Consequently, Malcolm writes letters to his relatives and friends back in the United States, to share his new-found spirit of unity and brotherhood.

Analysis

Malcolm's final spiritual journey takes place in this chapter. When he arrives in Jedda he is lonely and bewildered; he is unable to speak the language and is unfamiliar with the customs and traditions of the Muslim people. The metaphor he uses to describe his feelings in this situation suggests, symbolically, the imminent 'birth' of his new ideology. He says, "I never had felt more alone, and helpless, since I was a baby."

Throughout the chapter, the reader is deeply moved by Malcolm's passion as he describes the people and situations he encounters. When he is being driven to Mecca, for example, he says, "I was beyond astonishment....I was, all at once, thrilled, important, humble, and thankful."

Upon the completion of his pilgrimage, Malcolm dramatically announces his changing ideology and renounces his black separatist beliefs. He gains a new insight into the true religion of Islam,

describing the "color blindness of the Muslim world's religious and . . . human society." In a letter explaining his new ideas, Malcolm expresses his feelings about Mecca's "spirit of true brotherhood." He writes, "I have been utterly speechless and spellbound by the graciousness I see displayed all around me by people of all colors." He concludes, "All praise is due to Allah," and signs his letter with his new, Arabic name, "El-Hajj Malik El-Shabazz."

Study Questions

1. What does Dr. Shawarbi give Malcolm before his departure to Mecca?

2. The first city Malcolm visits in the Middle East is Cairo. Describe this city.

3. What is the literal meaning of Hajj in Arabic?

4. Malcolm learns that rugs play an important role in the Muslim culture. Name the five ways Muslims use these rugs.

5. What important ritual do Muslims practice before prayer?

6. Where does Malcolm stay when he is in Jedda?

7. Why is Malcolm amazed by the hospitality of Dr. Azzam and his family?

8. At the conclusion of Malcolm's pilgrimage to Mecca, where do he and his fellow pilgrims go?

9. What impresses Malcolm the most about his pilgrimage?

10. After his pilgrimage, to whom does Malcolm write?

Answers

1. Dr. Shawarbi gives Malcolm a letter of approval for his upcoming pilgrimage to Mecca. He also gives Malcolm a book, *The Eternal Message of Muhammad*, by Abd ir-Rahman Azzam.

2. Cairo is one of the most highly industrialized cities on the African continent. It has modern schools, housing developments, highways, and automobile and bus manufacturing industries.

3. The literal meaning of Hajj in Arabic is "to set out toward a definite objective."

4. Muslims use rugs to pray, eat, sit, sleep, as a courtroom, and as a classroom.

5. The important ritual Muslims practice before prayer is ablution, or washing one's body.

6. Malcolm stays in Mr. Azzam's suite in the Jedda Palace Hotel.

7. Malcolm is amazed by the hospitality of Dr. Azzam and his family because they are white, and he has never met Dr. Azzam or his family.

8. At the conclusion of his pilgrimage, Malcolm and the other pilgrims go to Mount Arafat to pray.

9. The strong sense of brotherhood that Malcolm feels throughout the pilgrimage impresses him the most.

10. After his pilgrimage, Malcolm writes to Betty, Ella, Dr. Shawarbi, Wallace Muhammad, and to his assistants at the Muslim Mosque, Inc.

Suggested Essay Topics

1. Malcolm's pilgrimage to Mecca consists of a series of rituals. Describe these rituals and the underlying significance of them in the Islamic religion.

2. Malcolm acknowledges that, "America needs to understand Islam, because this is the one religion that erases from its society the race problem." Explain this ideology.

Chapter 18: El-Hajj Malik El-Shabazz

New People:

Kasem Gulek: *member of the Turkish Parliament whom Malcolm meets on Mount Arafat*

Sheikh Abdullah Eraif: *mayor of Mecca*

Muhammad Abdul Azziz Maged: *Saudi Arabia's Deputy Chief of Protocol, who serves as an interpreter for conversations between Malcolm and Prince Faisal*

Professor Essien-Udom: *author of* Black Nationalism, *and a professor at Ibadan University in Lagos, Nigeria*

Larry Jackson: *black Peace Corps' volunteer whom Malcolm meets in Nigeria*

Julian Mayfield: *author and leader of Ghana's group of African-American expatriates*

Ana Livia: *Mayfield's wife*

Dr. Kwame Nkrumah: *President of Ghana*

Shirley Graham Du Bois: *writer and director of Ghanaian television; and widow of famous African-American revolutionary and scholar, Dr. W.E.B. Du Bois, who moved to Ghana late in his life*

Summary

Malcolm visits several Middle Eastern and African countries, and is introduced to the leaders, diplomats, and press corps from many nations. He meets the Saudi Arabian ruler, Prince Faisal, and Ghana's President, Dr. Nkrumah. He is treated with honor and respect wherever he travels.

Upon his return to New York, Malcolm holds an impromptu press conference to explain his new ideology. Although the news media reports are somewhat negative, Malcolm begins, for the first time in his life, to garner support from both white people and African-Americans. He is committed to developing political and so-

cial strategies that will unite all African-Americans in his fight against racism.

Analysis

The tremendously positive response Malcolm receives during his visit to Africa serves as an affirmation of his spiritual awakening.

He returns to the United States in May 1964. It is the beginning of a long, hot summer of racial unrest in many of America's major cities. Despite being cast by the news media as a "symbol" of the "revolt and violence" in the African-American community, Malcolm repudiates these charges. He launches into an attack of the American social and political systems that have denied "human rights" to African–Americans. He explains his new ideology, declaring, "My pilgrimage broadened my scope. It blessed me with a new insight. In two weeks in the Holy Land, I saw what I never had seen in thirty-nine years here in America. I saw all races, all colors—blue-eyed blonds to black-skinned Africans—in true brotherhood. In unity! Living as one!"

The reader marvels at this new Malcolm. Rather than merely spewing anger and hatred without taking action, Malcolm's focus has drastically shifted; he is now determined to develop practical, workable solutions to America's race problems.

Study Questions

1. What daily customs and routines does Malcolm begin to follow?

2. After his experiences, what recommendations does Malcolm have for African-American leaders?

3. Malcolm names two American authors who have "helped to spread and intensify the concern for the American black man." Who are they?

4. Why does Malcolm voice suspicion when he finds out the United States' State Department official, G. Mennen Williams, is visiting Africa?

5. In Lagos, Nigeria, Malcolm is given a new name by the Mus-

lim Students' Society. What is that name? Explain its significance.

6. What African country's wealth and natural beauty impresses Malcolm the most?

7. What other prominent African–American leader visited Ghana before Malcolm?

8. Compare Casablanca's famous Casbah with New York City's Harlem. How are they similar?

9. When Malcolm uses the word "Negro," he is corrected, and told to use the term "Afro-American" instead. Explain.

10. When asked about the reason for his split with Elijah Muhammad, what response does Malcolm give?

Answers

1. The Muslim customs that Malcolm begins to follow are ablutions before daily praying in a seated posture, in addition to eating from the same plates, drinking from the same glasses, and sleeping on the same rugs, with many people.

2. Malcolm recommends that African-American leaders travel extensively in non-white countries.

3. The two American authors whom Malcolm mentions are James Baldwin and John Griffin.

4. Malcolm voices his suspicions about G. Mennen Williams' visit to Africa because Williams was the Governor of Michigan when Malcolm's father was murdered, and nothing had ever been done about that crime.

5. Malcolm is given the name "Omowale" by the Muslim Students' Society. It means, in the Yoruba language, "the son who has come home."

6. Malcolm is most impressed with Ghana's wealth and natural beauty.

7. Dr. W.E.B. Du Bois visited Africa before Malcolm.

8. Casablanca's famous Casbah was once a ghetto for dark-

skinned native Moroccans, just as New York City's Harlem is a ghetto for African-Americans.

9. Malcolm is told that the term "Afro-American" has greater meaning and dignity than "Negro."

10. When asked about his split with Elijah Muhammad, Malcolm explains that they had disagreed about the political direction and involvement in African–Americans' struggle for human rights. He says that he respects the Nation of Islam as a "source of moral and social reform."

Suggested Essay Topics

1. What is a scapegoat? Malcolm refers to himself as a "scapegoat" during a conversation at Professor Essien-Udom's dinner party. Explain.

2. What are the attitudes of African black people toward African–Americans? How does Malcolm think African–American leaders can learn from their counterparts in Africa?

Chapter 19: 1965

Summary

In 1964, Malcolm embarks upon a large-scale campaign to gain support for his new organization. He holds public meetings and appears on numerous televison and radio programs. The American media continues its attack on Malcolm, calling him "the angriest Negro in America."

He revisits the Middle East and Africa, and has meetings with many world and religious leaders. Among the prominent world leaders with whom he has private audiences are President Gamal Abdel Nasser of Egypt; President Jomo Kenyatta, of Kenya; and Prime Minister Dr. Milton Obote of Uganda.

Upon his return to the United States, he continues his crusade to fight racism, renaming his organization the Organization of Afro-

American Unity. He begins reaching out to white Americans. He writes about his new insight, "the white man is not inherently evil, but American's racist society influences him to act evilly. The society has produced and nourishes a psychology which brings out the lowest, most base part of human beings." Malcolm advises, "Let sincere white individuals find all other white people they can who feel as they do—and let them form their own all-white groups, to work trying to convert other white people who are thinking and acting so racist. Let sincere whites go and teach non-violence to white people."

Toward the end of the chapter, Malcolm ominously predicts his own death. "I know that societies often have killed the people who have helped to change those societies," he declares. "And if I can die having brought any light, having exposed any meaningful truth that will help to destroy the racist cancer that is malignant in the body of America—then, all of the credit is due to Allah."

Analysis

In this final chapter of *The Autobiography of Malcolm X*, Malcolm emerges as a powerful, though tragic, figure. The reader is struck by the clear, matter-of-fact tone he uses as he describes the apprehensions he has about his own future, and prophesizes his death. He acknowledges, "Every morning when I wake up, now, I regard it as having another borrowed day. In any city...black men are watching every move I make, awaiting their chance to kill me. I have said publicly many times that I know that they have their orders."

Reflecting upon his life, Malcolm writes, "I believe that it would be almost impossible to find anywhere in America a black man who has lived further down in the mud of human society than I have . . . or a black man who has suffered more anguish during his life than I have. But it is only after the deepest darkness that the greatest joy can come; it is only after slavery and prison that the sweetest appreciation of freedom can come. . . . I do believe that I have fought the best that I knew how, and the best that I could." Unfortunately, most of what Malcolm predicts regarding how he will be perceived after his death has come true. He says, "I do not expect to live long enough to read this book in its finished form—

I want you to just watch and see if I'm not right in what I say: that the white man, in his press, is going to identify me with 'hate.'"

Finally, Malcolm explains his purpose in writing an autobiography, as he considers his experience to be a universal one among African–Americans. "It might prove to be a testimony of some social value. . . . " he writes. "I hope, that the objectve reader, in following my life—the life of only one ghetto-created Negro—may gain a better picture and understanding than he has previously had of the black ghettoes which are shaping the lives and the thinking of all of the 22 million Negroes who live in America."

Study Questions

1. Where does Malcolm hold many of his public meetings?

2. Malcolm cites two countries as having had a "revolution" to overthrow their old systems of leadership. What countries does he cite?

3. From where does the city of St. Augustine, Florida, get its name?

4. According to orthodox Muslim law, who was Muhammad ibn Adbullah?

5. While Malcolm is abroad in 1964, there is a campaign going on in the United States for President. Who are the two major candidates in that election?

6. What shocking F.B.I. statistic does Malcolm cite regarding crime in America?

7. What does Malcolm regret about his past?

8. What languages does Malcolm want to learn?

9. Which journalists does Malcolm consider to be "open and objective"?

10. If he is killed, whom does Malcolm think would be responsible?

Answers

1. Malcolm holds many of his public meetings in Harlem's Audubon Ballroom.

2. The two countries that Malcolm cites as having had a "revolution" to overthrow their old systems of leadership are Egypt and Algeria.

3. St. Augustine, Florida, "is named for the black African saint who saved Catholicism from heresy."

4. According to orthodox Muslim law, Muhammad ibn Abdullah lived in the Holy City of Mecca 1400 years ago. He was the last Messenger of Allah.

5. The two major candidates in the 1964 United States presidential election are Lyndon Johnson and Barry Goldwater.

6. Malcolm cites a shocking F.B.I. statistic regarding the rising crime rate in the United States. Since the end of World War II, statistics indicate that there has been an annual 10 to 12 percent rise in the crime rate.

7. Malcolm regrets that he never received a good academic education.

8. Malcolm wants to learn the basic African dialects, Chinese, and Arabic.

9. Malcolm considers Irv Kupcinet in Chicago, and Barry Farber, Barry Gray, and Mike Wallace in New York to be "open and objective."

10. Malcolm thinks he will be killed by the Muslims from the Nation of Islam.

Suggested Essay Topics

1. Malcolm compares the American Indians' experiences with the African-Americans' experiences. How are these two situations similar?

2. Describe Malcolm X's complex attitude toward Jewish people.

Epilogue by Alex Haley

New People:

Alex Haley: *the person to whom Malcolm tells his autobiography, and writer of the autobiography's epilogue*

Ossie Davis: *popular actor and friend of Malcolm, who eulogized Malcolm*

Reverend Milton Galamison: *militant clergyman, who was scheduled to be the co-speaker with Malcolm at the Audubon Ballroom on the day Malcolm was assassinated*

Brother Benjamin X: *Malcolm's assistant at the Muslim Mosque, Inc.*

Stanley Scott: *United Press International reporter who was at the Audubon Ballroom when Malcolm was assassinated*

Bishop Alvin A. Childs: *Malcolm's funeral was held at his church, Church of God in Christ*

Summary

In this chapter, Alex Haley traces his two-year association with Malcolm X. Initially, Malcolm was reluctant to reveal intimate details about his past to Haley. However, Haley's thoughtful, probing questions soon put Malcolm at ease. Haley uncovers Malcolm X—the child, the criminal, and finally, the dynamic, influential political activist and African-American leader. Haley spends countless hours with Malcolm, and the two men develop a close friendship. Malcolm shares his concerns about his premonition of death at the hands of followers of the Nation of Islam.

Haley offers a detailed account of the events following Malcolm's assassination at the Audubon Ballroom on February 21, 1965. After being shot 16 times, Malcolm was taken to Columbia-Presbyterian Hospital. He was dead upon arrival.

Several Harlem churches turned down requests to allow his funeral to take place on their premises. The funeral was held at

Harlem's Church of God in Christ. Bishop Childs, who officiated at the funeral service, received numerous bomb threats at his church and his home.

Prominent African-Americans expressed their remorse upon learning about the death of Malcolm X, including Dr. Kenneth B. Clark, a famous psychologist; James Baldwin, an author and dramatist; Dr. Martin Luther King, Jr., a popular civil rights leader; James Farmer, CORE's (Congress of Racial Equality) National Director; and a large number of national and international leaders.

Analysis

The Epilogue gives the reader a unique opportunity to gain insight into the thought processes of Malcolm during the creation of his autobiography. Malcolm's honesty and candor with Haley is evident throughout.

Haley had great respect and admiration for Malcolm. His final comments effectively sum up the book. He says, "I tried to be a dispassionate chronicler. But he was the most electric personality I have ever met, and I still can't quite conceive him dead. It still feels to me as if he has just gone into some next chapter, to be written by historians."

Study Questions

1. In what national publications do articles about Elijah Muhammad's Nation of Islam first appear?

2. What was Malcolm's first reaction to Alex Haley's proposal about the publication of his life story?

3. What does Haley first ask Malcolm about that induces Malcolm to reveal intimate details about his life?

4. Next to college, where does Malcolm think is "the best place for a man to go if he needs to do some thinking"?

5. According to Haley, what is Malcolm's opinion of Dr. Martin Luther King, Jr.?

6. By Malcolm's calculations, what was the Nation of Islam's membership before he joined? What was the membership 12 years later?

7. What are the goals of Malcolm's new organization, the OAAU (Organization of Afro-American Unity)?

8. A *New York Times'* opinion poll questioned New York City's African-Americans about their opinions on black leaders. What were the results of that poll?

9. Haley reports that Harlem's residents were complaining about Malcolm X. What were their complaints?

10. When does an orthodox Moslem funeral service take place? Explain.

Answers

1. Articles about Elijah Muhammad's Nation of Islam first appeared in *Reader's Digest,* the *Saturday Evening Post,* and *Playboy* magazine.

2. Malcolm is startled and uncertain when Haley proposes to write his life story.

3. Haley asks Malcolm about his mother, which induces Malcolm to reveal intimate details about his life.

4. Malcolm thinks that "the best place for a man to go if he needs to do some thinking" is prison.

5. Malcolm had "reluctant admiration" for Dr. Martin Luther King, Jr.

6. Before he joined, Malcolm calculates that the Nation of Islam had 400 members. Twelve years later, Malcolm calculates that the membership is around 40,000.

7. The goals of Malcolm's new organization, OAAU (Organization of Afro-American Unity) is "to unite Afro-Americans for a constructive program toward attainment of human rights." In addition, it seeks "to convert the Negro population from non-violence to active self-defense against white supremacists across America."

8. A *New York Times'* poll of African-Americans finds "three-fourths had named Dr. Martin Luther King as 'doing the best work for Negroes,'" and "one-fifth had voted for N.A.A.C.P.'s

Roy Wilkins, while only six percent had voted for Malcolm
X."

9. Harlems' residents were complaining about Malcolm X because they felt that all he actually did was talk, and not take
action. In addition, they felt that he was often confused and
that he changed his opinions easily.

10. An orthodox Moslem funeral service takes place within 48
hours of a person's death. Moslems believed that "when a
body grows cold the soul leaves it and when the body is put
into the earth it comes alive again."

Suggested Essay Topics

1. How does Malcolm feel about his past—his days as a street
hustler, thief, and prisoner? What lasting impact does he feel
these prior experiences had on his life?

2. The relationship that Malcolm X and Alex Haley had was a
complex one. Why was Malcolm initially reluctant to reveal
himself to Haley? What caused Malcolm to "warm up" to
Haley? Describe the evolution of their relationship.

3. What events occur—that are unrelated to Malcolm X—during the writing of the autobiography that chronicle the racial climate of America in the early 1960s?

On Malcolm X by Ossie Davis

Summary and Analysis

Actor Ossie Davis eulogized Malcolm X at his funeral. He writes
this short essay in response to a magazine editor's question, "Why
did you eulogize Malcolm X?"

To Davis, Malcolm represented "refreshing excitement." He
considered Malcolm "one of the most fascinating and charming
men I have ever met," and a "hero." He admired and was intrigued

by Malcolm's relentless energy. "He [Malcolm X] kept shouting the painful truth we whites and blacks did not want to hear from all the housetops. And he wouldn't stop for love nor money."

Davis thinks Malcolm was "a true man." He concedes, however, that "to protect my relations with the many good white folks who make it possible for me to earn a fairly good living . . . I was too chicken, too cautious, to admit that fact when he was alive."

The reader marvels at this mainstream African-American actor's honesty. How will Malcolm X be perceived by future generations of Americans? Davis' response, "I am content to wait for history to make the final decision."

Sample Analytical Paper Topics

The following paper topics are designed to test your understanding of the autobiography as a whole and to analyze important themes. Following each question is a sample outline to help you get started.

Topic #1

What long range effects did the death of Reverend Little, Malcolm's father, have on Malcolm?

Outline

I. Thesis Statement: *Malcolm was only eight years old when his father was brutally murdered. Throughout his life, he was looking for a father figure to make up for his earlier, tragic loss.*

II. Father Figures

   A. Mr. Ostrowski

   B. Hymie

   C. Bimbi

   D. The Honorable Elijah Mohammad

   E. Allah, the Muslim God

III. Father Figures' Contributions to Malcolm

   A. Mr. Ostrowski initially encouraged Malcolm in school

   B. Bimbi encouraged Malcolm to take prison correspondence courses

    C. The Honorable Elijah Muhammad is instrumental in Malcolm's transformation

    D. Malcolm credits Allah with all of his success

Topic #2

What are Malcolm's views on women?

Outline

I.   Thesis Statement: *Malcolm was seriously disappointed by women early in his life. His process of spiritual transformation enabled him to regain his trust and confidence in women.*

II.   Malcolm's Early Experiences With Women

    A. His mother was unable to support and care for her family after her husband's murder

    B. Ella contrasts sharply with his mother

III. Malcolm's Later Experiences With Women

    A. Malcolm has little respect for Laura

    B. Sophia, as a white woman, represented the unattainable to Malcolm

    C. Ironically, Malcolm trusts the various prostitutes he meets

IV. Malcolm's Adulthood

    A. Malcolm slowly gains complete trust and confidence in Betty Shabazz

    B. Malcolm accepts Ella's generosity

    C. As a result, he reconciles with his mother

Topic #3

The theme of racial prejudice is evident throughout the book. How does Malcolm's autobiography reflect the racial prejudice of that time?

Outline

I. Thesis Statement: *Malcolm, his black family and his friends were denied equal treatment because of racial prejudice*

II. Father's Murder

    A. Killed by a local racist group

III. Malcolm's Academic Career

    A. He feels like he is treated like a "mascot"

    B. Excels in school, but was dissuaded from seeking a white-collar profession

IV. Boston and New York Experiences

    A. Bad influences of black ghetto life are pervasive—drugs, alcohol, gambling, and criminal activity

    B. West Indian Archie is a black street hustler, but has an extraordinary skill—photographic memory

V. Prison

    A. As a black man, Malcolm was given a stiffer sentence because he had white female friends

    B. Charlestown State Prison, with its largely black inmate population, offered virtually no rehabilitative services

VI. Minister Malcolm X

    A. White majority sought to discredit the Nation of Islam

VII. Malcolm's Ouster from the Nation of Islam

    A. White-controlled media continued to discredit Malcolm, despite his new ideology.

Bibliography

Quotations from *The Autobiography of Malcolm X* are taken from the following edition:

Malcolm X. *The Autobiography of Malcolm X as told to Alex Haley.* New York: Ballantine Books, 1964.

Other Sources:

Breitman, George, ed. (with prefatory notes). *Malcolm X Speaks: Selected Speeches and Statements.* New York: Grove Press Inc., 1966.

Haskins, James, *Profiles in Black Power.* Garden City, New York: Doubleday & Company, Inc., 1972.

NOTES

NOTES

NOTES

NOTES

NOTES

NOTES

NOTES

NOTES

NOTES

NOTES

REA's Study Guides

Review Books, Refreshers, and Comprehensive References

Problem Solvers®
Presenting an answer to the need for easy-to-understand study guides detailing the wide world of mathematics and science.

High School Tutors®
In-depth guides that cover the science and math subjects taught in high schools.

Essentials®
An insightful series of useful, practical, and informative references covering popular subjects.

Super Reviews®
Don't miss a thing! Review it all with this series of subject references at an affordable price.

Interactive Flashcard Books®
Flip through these essential, interactive study aids that go far beyond ordinary flashcards.

ESL
Easy-to-use reference for anyone who is learning the English language and wants to improve listening, speaking and writing skills.

For our complete title list, visit www.rea.com

Research & Education Association

REA's Test Preps

The Best in Test Preparation

Some of our titles include:

Advanced Placement Exams (APs)
Art History
Biology
Calculus AB & BC
Chemistry
Economics
English Language & Composition
English Literature & Composition
Environmental Science
European History
French Language
Government & Politics
Human Geography
Physics
Psychology
Spanish Language
Statistics
United States History
World History

College-Level Examination Program (CLEP)
American Government
American Literature
Biology
Calculus
Chemistry
College Algebra
College Composition
History of the United States I + II
Human Growth and Development
Introduction to Educational Psychology
Introductory Psychology

Introductory Sociology
Natural Sciences
Principles of Management
Principles of Marketing
Principles of Microeconomics
Spanish
Western Civilization I
Western Civilization II

SAT Subject Tests
Biology E/M
Chemistry
Latin
Literature
Mathematics Level 2
Spanish
United States History
World History

ACCUPLACER

ACT - ACT Assessment

ASVAB - Armed Services Vocational Aptitude Battery

CBEST - California Basic Educational Skills Test

CDL - Commercial Driver License Exam

COMPASS

COOP, HSPT & TACHS - Catholic High School Admission Tests

EMT

ESL

FTCE - Florida Teacher Certification Examinations

GED® Test

GMAT - Graduate Management Admission Test

GRE - Graduate Record Exams

LSAT - Law School Admission Test

MAT - Miller Analogies Test

MTEL - Massachusetts Tests for Educator Licensure

NCLEX

NYSTCE - New York State Teacher Certification Examinations

PRAXIS

SAT

TEAS

TExES - Texas Examinations of Educator Standards

TOEFL - Test of English as a Foreign Language

Research & Education Association